THE NATURAL WATER GARDEN

Pools, Ponds,
Marshes & Bogs
for Backyards
Everywhere

C. Colston Burrell ⁄ Guest Editor

Left: Swamp milkweed, *Asclepias incarnata*, is a magnet for butterflies.

Cover: Yellow skunk cabbage, *Lysichiton americanus*

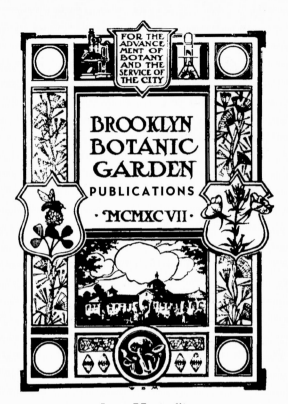

FOR THE ADVANCE MENT OF BOTANY AND THE SERVICE OF THE CITY

BROOKLYN BOTANIC GARDEN PUBLICATIONS ·MCMXCVII·

Janet Marinelli
SERIES EDITOR

Carol Goodstein
ASSOCIATE EDITOR

Bekka Lindstrom
ART DIRECTOR

Stephen K-M. Tim
VICE PRESIDENT, SCIENCE, LIBRARY & PUBLICATIONS

Judith D. Zuk
PRESIDENT

Elizabeth Scholtz
DIRECTOR EMERITUS

Handbook #151

Copyright © Summer 1997 by the Brooklyn Botanic Garden, Inc.

Handbooks in the 21st-Century Gardening Series, formerly Plants & Gardens,

are published quarterly at 1000 Washington Ave., Brooklyn, NY 11225.

Subscription included in Brooklyn Botanic Garden subscriber membership dues ($35.00 per year).

ISSN # 0362-5850 ISBN # 1-889538-01-9

Printed by Science Press, a division of the Mack Printing Group

CH 9/97

Table of Contents

The Natural Water Garden

BY C. COLSTON BURRELL

MY MOST MEMORABLE wetland experience ever was on a floating mat of sphagnum moss in a quaking bog in Maine. I had walked out through a veil of spruce lining the basin's perimeter onto a vast, undulating mat of red and green sphagnum. The moss stretched out as far as I could see, interrupted only by clumps of spruce that huddled together on elevated hummocks. Standing amidst that seemingly infinite, trackless bog, I felt dwarfed.

When I finally glanced down at my feet, I discovered that I was surrounded by the two carnivorous plants I had come to see. Partially buried in the lush moss were the blood-red, water-filled vessels of the purple pitcher plant. Carpeting the ground around them lay the dewdrop-studded leaves of the sundew. Like flypaper traps, these tiny plants were lying in wait for the slightest movement of a gnat to trigger their dew-drenched tentacles into motion and finally push the struggling insect down onto the leaf, supplying it with valuable nitrogen.

It was the mysterious allure of these unique plants that led me as a boy to that enchanted place in Maine. Once there, however, I also discovered delicate arethusa and grass pink orchids, floating branches of horned bladderwort and shrubs with leather-like leaves, including leatherleaf and bog rosemary.

Often, it takes an initial connection to an orchid, a bird or a plant to inspire a person's appreciation of wetlands. Once appreciated, it's more likely that wetlands will be preserved. Wetland gardening is another way of bringing people

Wetlands are home to a host of fascinating plants, such as the carnivorous California pitcher plant, *Darlingtonia californica.*

into contact with the plants and animals that make up these vital ecosystems.

To untrained eyes, wetlands look messy and chaotic. Rank growth and the threat of mosquitoes contribute to the general perception that wetlands are an eyesore and a nuisance. Therefore, when designing wetland gardens, it is important to give them a cultural and aesthetic context, to make these landscapes more accessible to people who are unfamiliar with them. Cultural context can be provided by including familiar, colorful flowers such as iris, or by recognizable planting patterns such as bands or rows. It is also important to establish discernible boundaries between the wetland garden and the rest of the garden.

Why is it so critical for people to appreciate and preserve wetlands? Ecologically, wetlands are essential for several reasons: As habitats, they are home to an extraordinary array of species, including birds such as bitterns and wrens and animals including mink, otter, frogs, turtles, butterflies and dragonflies. They are also nature's flood-control systems.When dispersed properly throughout an ecosystem, wetlands can soak up excess water produced by storms and gradually release it, thereby reducing or eliminating flooding. Where wetlands are filled in and paved over, flood waters run quickly over the impervious landscape, gathering volume and power as they go. When this concentrated water finally reaches streams and rivers, it can cause them to flood. What's more, by collecting water that would otherwise run off into streams and rivers, wetlands also replen-

By mimicking the structure and functions of a native wetland, you can create a garden that is beautiful, biodiverse and easy to maintain.

ish aquifers and groundwater supplies.

The Natural Water Garden takes an ecological design approach to water gardening. It focuses on methods of mimicking the structure and functions of natural wetland systems and creating residential water gardens that are both biodiverse and easy to maintain. "Wetland Ecology for Gardeners" introduces the wetland ecosystem, discusses the structure and function of wetlands and describes how you can use this information as a basis for your own natural water garden. "Constructing a Wetland Garden," "Pools & Ponds" and "A Bog Garden" are among the chapters that offer practical tips and techniques for building ecological water gardens, along with specific case studies of various types of backyard wetlands. Finally, this handbook provides recommendations for plants best suited to specific wetland types and sites around the country.

There is one caveat even for gardeners taking an ecological approach: Wetlands are protected ecosystems, generally under state jurisdiction. Before making any alterations to an existing wetland on your property, check with the appropriate state agency, usually the department of natural resources or environment.

When you bring water into the landscape, you add more than an aesthetic flourish. You create an ecosystem. With care, that ecosystem can both thrive and inspire appreciation. In time, a chorus of spring peepers, the glint of gossamer dragonfly wings — and the knowledge that you are helping the environment — will justly reward your efforts.

Wetland Ecology for Gardeners

BY LESLIE YETKA AND SUSAN GALATOWITSCH

TYPICALLY, we experience wetlands from a distance — as casual spectators from a boardwalk, boat or a ridge — because being *in* a wetland means sinking into ooze, precariously hopping from one clump of tangled roots to another, slogging through dense vegetation and, of course, fending off pesky mosquitoes. However, careful observation of wetlands reveals a distinctive combination of water, soil and plants that harbors a great variety of species unable to exist in any other type of habitat. Familiarizing yourself with the ecology of these habitats, learning how the water, plants and topography of native wetlands interact, is the first step in restoring or creating a wetland garden.

THE MOVEMENT OF WATER

To truly understand wetlands and wetland plants, you first need to know a bit about hydrology, or the movement of water. Water creates wetlands, and you usually will find wetlands where water accumulates at a rate faster than it drains away. As you visit different wetlands, you will notice that some are inundated year-round while others are not, that some are shallow and others are deep. For example, the otherwise dry lands of California's mountain valleys are occasionally punctuated by shallow depressions that hold water for brief periods in the spring. When these vernal pools fill after heavy rains or snowmelt, they erupt

In arid areas, cottonwoods grow in wetlands along arroyos and streams.

Skunk cabbage, *Symplocarpus foetidus*, thrives in a swamp in New York State.

WETLAND TYPES

Marsh: Supports soft-stemmed herbaceous plants including grasses, sedges and reeds.

Swamp: A closed-canopy wetland dominated by woody plants: flood-tolerant trees and shrubs.

Bog: Characterized by high acidity, poor drainage, sphagnum mosses and peat.

with aquatic plant and animal life. Eventually, the water evaporates into the atmosphere or percolates down through the soil, recharging the groundwater. Any seeds that have been dropped by the plants become dormant until the next rainfall fills up the pool again. At lower elevations, this groundwater may again reach the surface as springs or seeps, providing a steady supply of water to wetlands year-round.

Other wetlands are created by the regular ebb and flow of rivers, lakes and oceans. Whereas coastal wetlands are affected by the twice daily tides, lit-

Blue flag iris blooms in a northern swamp dominated by sedges.

Glacial lakes and bogs are common in the northern states and Canada.

toral or lake-edge wetlands also experience a regular rise and fall of water levels. Floodplains, the low-lying lands along rivers, often flood after heavy storms. Even after most of the water has receded to the main waterways, some may remain trapped in the lower depressions of these floodplains. Thus, water can remain close to the surface year-round, supporting extensive forests along with pockets of emergent wetland vegetation such as cattails and arrowhead. Shrubs, including buttonbush and willows, grow as a fringe along the river channel. Periodic flooding along the Mississippi River supports floodplain wetlands from temperate Minnesota all the way down to subtropical Louisiana.

WETLAND PLANTS

As wetlands flood, soil microbes quickly deplete oxygen in the soil, using it, as we do, to respire. In flooded soils, upland plants cannot get the oxygen they need. However, wetland plants are able to cope with this by producing large, interconnected cells called aerenchyma that extend from the shoots to the roots.

Acting like straws, these chains of cells flush oxygen down to the roots of the plant, creating an oxygenated environment for them. By splitting lengthwise the leaves of thick-stemmed plants like cattails and bul-rushes, you can easily see these air chambers.

Even with their special adaptations to flooding, individual species of wet-land plants have differing limits as to the depth of water they can tolerate. A plant's ability to tolerate a certain water depth is what determines its zone (see opposite page). Wet mead-ow zone species, including *Carex lanuginosa* and swamp milkweed *(Asclepias incarnata),* thrive best in soils that undergo alternating wet and dry periods. Sedges and other small perennials, including marsh marigolds, tend to be located at the

Plants like cattails can survive in wet-lands because they have "air chambers" that deliver oxygen to their roots.

water's edge where they remain wet throughout the growing season. Emergent zone plants such as cattails and bulrushes are best suited to persistent flooding; just enough of the leaves need to remain above the water to photosynthesize sugars for the entire plant. The leaves of floating and submersed aquatics such as water-lilies and pondweeds photosynthesize in water, enabling them to live in deep water, beyond the reach of even the tallest emergents. These species are so suited to growing in deep water that their stems lack the strength to hold the plant upright without the support of the surrounding water. Submersed aquatics can grow in shallower water if emergent aquatics and suspended particles have not diminished light penetrating the water.

WATER CHEMISTRY AND PLANT LIFE

Wetlands differ not only in water quantity but also in chemistry. Wetland waters range from alkaline to acid, depending on groundwater and organic substrate.

continued on page 12

WETLAND ZONES

Wetland plants are typically arranged in a series of concentric bands or zones determined by water depth. Plants that are able to tolerate similar depths of water grow in similar zones.

The *wet meadow zone* is found where the wetland grades into upland. It regularly undergoes periods of wet and dry. Depending on where in the country a wetland is located, the wet meadow zone may be dominated by emergent plants or shrubs and trees.

Adjacent to the wet meadow zone lies the *emergent zone*, dominated by soft-stemmed, herbaceous plants that grow partially in water. Most of the time, their roots are submerged and their leaves and stems are exposed to light and air. Emergent species include cattails, pickerel weed, arrowheads, bulrush, grasses and sedges.

Submersed aquatics and *floating plants* like water-lilies, water hyacinths and pondweeds are found in deep water. Their leaves are capable of photosynthesizing under water.

UPLAND

WET MEADOW ZONE

EMERGENT ZONE

DEEP WATER

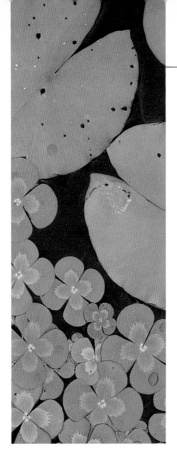

Floating plants like water-lily and water clover live in deep water, beyond the reach of even the tallest emergents.

Because bogs receive water directly from rainfall rather than from surface runoff or groundwater, they are mineral-poor and acidic. Acid-loving plants such as the common pitcher plant (*Sarracenia purpurea*) and sphagnum moss (*Sphagnum* spp.) thrive in these acidic conditions.

As water flows through the ground, soil minerals and nutrients are dissolved and transported into wetlands, resulting in a high mineral content or alkaline condition. Called fens, these wetlands harbor a distinct group of species known as calciphiles. For example, grass-of-Parnassus (*Parnassia glauca*) and sterile sedge (*Carex sterilis*) are abundant in fens but rare elsewhere. Alkaline wetlands are also common in arid regions such as the Great Plains and the Desert Southwest, where water from surface runoff (rather than groundwater) evaporates, leaving behind dissolved minerals. Only a few salt-loving plants, such as saltgrass (*Distichlis spicata*), are able to withstand these conditions. They either prevent salt from entering their roots, or are able to excrete it through nodules. Known as halophytes, these plants tend to have thick stems and cuticles, wax-like substances on their leaves that prevent excessive water loss.

VITAL DISTURBANCES

Disturbances like hurricanes and floods can be catastrophic for cities and farms. However, many wetland ecosystems are not only resilient to periodic disturbances but dependent on them. For example, the floodplains of rivers in the western United States used to support stands of cottonwood trees, which are now declining. The cottonwoods rely on spring flooding for the germination of their seeds. However, once irrigation reservoirs were built to capture winter snowmelt, the floods ceased and so did cottonwood regeneration.

Severe droughts can also rejuvenate some wetlands. Emergent plants of prairie wetlands germinate on wet, not saturated soils. Only during severe

Many wetland plants, such as those that live in the floodplains along rivers, depend on periodic flooding.

droughts, which occur every ten to fifteen years, does water in large, deep marshes draw down to expose saturated mudflats. Seeds stored in the soil seedbank germinate on the mudflats. These plants grow and expand when precipitation returns. As their populations increase, they attract muskrats, which graze on the emergent plants faster than the plants can make new shoots. The marsh then becomes lake-like until the next drought.

Some types of wetlands are more resilient to disturbances — both natural and human — than others. Wetlands fed by precipitation tend to be less sensitive to perturbation because they are accustomed to fluctuating water levels throughout their growing season. On the other hand, bogs and fens — wetlands fed by groundwater — are more sensitive to disturbances. These wetlands harbor plant communities that have stabilized over a significant period of time. In some northern wetlands, the accumulation of undecomposed organic matter, known as peat, can be over 10 meters thick and 10,000 years old. They often support sensitive and slow-growing rare plant species with low reproductive rates, including orchids, lilies and irises. Even minor changes in hydrology can have a severe

The patterns of vegetation of any wetland determine to a great extent the types of wildlife that visit it. Waterfowl and shorebirds, such as this great blue heron, tend to forage in the shallow water and nest in the tall vegetation along the water's edge.

impact. If these wetlands are artificially drained, the peat rapidly decomposes and the land can actually drop significantly, cracking with fissures up to 100 feet deep.

In urban areas, stormwater flows to man-made wetlands may be similar in timing to natural wetlands but dramatically different in magnitude. For instance, an undisturbed wetland without stormwater drainage may experience about a foot of change in water depth a year. An urban wetland, by comparison, may suddenly rise three or four feet due to runoff from streets, roofs, concrete and other impermeable surfaces. This dramatic rise in water level may be more than some plants can tolerate.

Fertilizer is another human-introduced disturbance that can harm wetlands. Fertilizers applied to lawns are often lost to surface runoff, and eventually end up in wetlands. Certain wetland plants, such as cattails, thrive on this fertilization and grow at the expense of others. The result is a wetland with very few species.

Although garden wetlands typically are not as sensitive to periodic climatic dis-

When you create a wetland garden, you should model it after local sites with soil and other conditions similar to those on your property.

turbances as natural wetlands are, wetland gardeners should mimic natural disturbances as much as possible. For example, it is not a good idea to add water at a time in the natural cycle when the water should be down because germination may be adversely affected.

THE RIGHT WETLANDS FOR YOUR REGION

Various combinations of geology, precipitation and temperature result in a rich diversity of wetlands. For example, sedge meadows are native only to the temperate north, while riparian desert forests with cottonwoods (*Populus* spp.) and saltbush (*Artiplex* spp.) are uniquely found along rivers in arid regions. When preparing to restore or create a wetland, be sure to visit healthy wetlands in parks, wildlife refuges or preserves in your area. Look at sites with conditions similar to those on your property and plan to mimic both species composition and vegetation zones (see page 11). Notice the arrangement of plants. In many wetlands, the organization of vegetation indicates the flooding patterns. Over the years, the bands or zones of emergent, floating and submersed aquatics may migrate up and down a shoreline, depending on water-level fluctuations. Extensive shallow wetlands with little topographical change, such as sedge meadows, have fairly uniform mixtures of plants.

Ask the site manager or a local naturalist about the hydrology of any wetland you are planning to use as a model. You need to know whether your wetland will rely on surface runoff or groundwater flow. Then be sure that these water sources that were historically important have not been diverted or obstructed by roads, ditches or filling. Consult your county soil conservationist to help you determine how similar the soil on your property is to the the soil in the wetland you are using as your model. Similar soils bode well for the success of your wetland project because you can be reasonably certain that the plants you have chosen will find the nutrients, texture and water conditions suitable.

The patterns of vegetation, or lack thereof, at any wetland site greatly determine the types of wildlife that visit it. Waterfowl and shorebirds tend to forage in shallow water and nest in tall vegetation found along the water's edge. Mammals such as muskrats and beavers find materials for dens and food reserves in forested wetlands. Wetland vegetation provides habitat for insects and amphibians, which in turn provide food for other wildlife.

KEEPING OUT INVADERS

Unfortunately, wetlands support more than their fair share of invasive species. Purple loosestrife (*Lythrum salicaria*), reed canary grass (*Phalaris arundinacea*), hybrid cattail *(Typha* x *glauca)*, tamarisks (*Tamarix chinensis, T. parviflora* and *T. ramosissima*), glossy buckthorn (*Rhamnus frangula*)and water hyacinth *(Eichhornia crassipes)* are just a few examples of the rapacious plants that can overrun a wetland if not kept in check. Some species, like purple loosestrife, were deliberately introduced for their horticultural value. Some, like hybrid cattail, have become invasive because they can tolerate pollution such as road salt and fertilizer.

Invasive species can spread rapidly and eventually replace all the native vegetation in a habitat. Large stands of any single plant reduce the species diversity, as well as alter ecosystem processes such as the frequency of wildfires, the availability of water or nutrients and the rate of soil erosion — ultimately resulting in habitat loss. While the federal Clean Water Act has slowed the draining and filling of wetlands, it does not regulate habitat loss due to invasive species. Therefore, thousands of acres of American wetlands are lost each year due to plant invaders.

Newly replanted wetlands are particularly vulnerable to invasives because these aggressive species are typically good colonizers of open sites. The best way to keep them out of your wetland is to pull out the plants by hand, including the roots, as they colonize. Never let invasives seed. Large populations of invasives often can be controlled only by chemical herbicides.

Knowing which species are native to wetlands in your area is an essential part of reducing habitat loss from invasive species. Some invasive exotics are available commercially. Don't buy them — even if growers claim they are so-called infertile strains; studies have shown that purple loosestrife cultivars claimed to be infertile, for example, are not. It's generally wise to avoid non-native species in your wetland garden. A gardening experiment with an exotic aquatic could be the cause of our next serious wetland invader.

Freshwater Wetlands of North America

F YOU HAVE EVER SEEN the vast marshlands of South Dakota's prairie potholes covered in a sea of ice, paddled through a foggy marsh at sunrise or listened to the throaty call of a bullfrog, you will no doubt agree that wetlands harbor a still serenity that makes them truly remarkable places — far different from their reputation as mosquito-ridden, malaria-infested, mucky, murky mires. This common misperception has led to their widespread demise. Until very recently, wetlands were drained or filled, farmed or paved over. Of the 215 million acres of wetlands that existed in the contiguous forty-eight states a couple of hundred years ago, only 99 million acres remain.

Despite their widespread devastation, you still can find freshwater wetlands in every region of this continent. Inland marshes, the most widely and evenly distributed, are characterized by predominantly herbaceous sun-loving plants and a few shrubs. They range from the sawgrass marshes of Florida's Everglades (the largest marsh complex in the United States) to the northern marshes of New England, home to great blue herons, moose and muskrats. The largest concentration of inland marshes is found in the prairie pothole region, extending from the north-central United States into south-central Canada. These vast grasslands are peppered with thousands of depressions formed 10,000 years ago, during the last Ice Age.

Peatlands — wetlands where organic matter decomposes more slowly than it is produced — occur most commonly in the northern U.S. and Canada. Peatlands include bogs, which often are blanketed with soft, spongy sphagnum mosses and

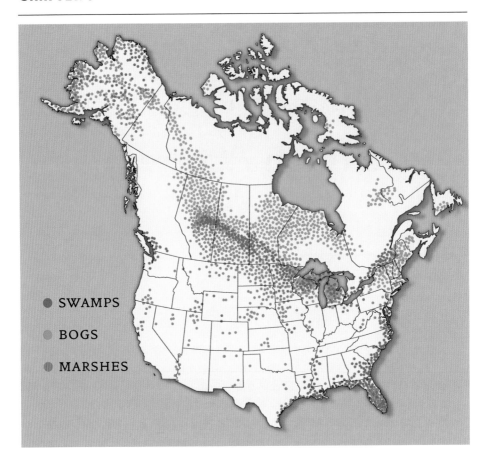

SWAMPS

BOGS

MARSHES

receive moisture mainly through precipitation, and fens, seepage sites with an internal flow of groundwater, which are dominated by sedges and shrubs and commonly host wildflowers such as white lady slipper, shrubby cinquefoil and fringed gentian. The northern or boreal peatlands are most widespread in Canada and Alaska. In fact, Canada has the highest concentration of peatlands in the world, more than 600,000 square miles. These boreal wetlands also occur regularly throughout Minnesota and Maine, with smaller pockets in the Pacific Northwest, the western mountains and the Appalachian Mountains in West Virginia.

Swamps — wetlands with shady canopies of trees or shrubs — include the tupelo and Spanish moss-laden cypress swamps of the South; the floodplain swamps of the Mississippi Valley; the towering pine pocosins of the Southeast; the red maple swamps of the East; and the black spruce, tamarack and cedar swamps of the northern U.S. and Canada.

Constructing a Wetland Garden

BY JUDY GLATTSTEIN

WETLANDS ON YOUR PROPERTY can be a boon or a bane. To non-gardeners they may be viewed as problems, areas that once would have been ditched and drained. Yet for eager gardeners, water presents so many compelling possibilities that those who lack natural wetlands on their property often create them.

A constructed wetland offers several advantages over a naturally occurring one. First, because a garden is not considered a naturally occurring habitat, altering it does not require local, state or federal permits. Secondly, you are not limited by nature — you can place the wetland wherever you want it. Third, you can design the wetland of your choice. Water gardening need not be restricted to ponds and water-lilies. Sunny areas with wet soil provide ideal habitat for marsh and wet-meadow plants, while shady sites offer opportunities for growing swamp plants.

Pre-formed pools, flexible liners and even whiskey barrels offer umpteen wetland possibilities for the do-it-yourself water gardener. All you need to know is how to wield a shovel. In fact, if all you want is a water garden on your terrace or patio, all you need is a container and a hose to fill it — forget the shovel.

The familiar half-whiskey barrel doesn't have to be planted with prosaic petunias. It can become a miniature pond or, sunk into the ground, can support wet meadow or swamp plants.

WHISKEY BARREL WETLAND

The familiar half-whiskey barrel, routinely planted with prosaic petunias, can easily become a small pond. If your barrel has drain holes, fill them with aquarium-grade caulking, or obtain an appropriately sized liner from a specialty water garden nursery. If the half-barrel has no drainage holes, you either can add a liner or prepare the barrel for direct use by scrubbing its interior using a stiff-bristled brush and plain water. Rinse three or four times and fill the half-barrel, allowing its staves to swell until water-tight. Remember that water is heavy, so place the container on a sturdy, level surface before filling it. Empty the half-barrel using a length of hose as a siphon, then fill it again. This sort of set-up is useful for water-lilies and emergent wetland plants.

Another option is to sink the half-barrel into the ground, perhaps leaving a couple of inches protruding as a decorative edge that also helps keep litter from blowing in. Keep in mind, though, that the half-barrel will last longer set on a terrace or patio than it will sunk into soil, where the staves will decay in a few years.

A third option is to caulk the bottom holes and drill a couple of drainage holes about halfway down the side of the half-barrel, through the widest staves. Filled with soil and placed in sun or shade, you now have a suitable container for marsh, wet meadow or swamp plants.

FIBERGLASS POOLS

Like a whiskey barrel, a preformed, rigid, fiberglass pool is also relatively simple to install. Pools are available in shapes ranging from round, rectangular or kidney-shaped to more free-form designs, and capacities that hold from 65 gallons up to 550 gallons. The smaller pools are generally 11 inches deep; the larger ones between 15 and 17 inches deep. Like the half-barrels, these smaller pools are adequate for water-lilies, which tolerate 6- to 18-inch deep water.

If your barrel has drainage holes, fill them with aquarium-grade caulking, or obtain a small-sized liner from a nursery that sells supplies for water gardens.

21

Choose a site in full view from your terrace, deck, patio, living room or other important room in the house. Place the pool at the toe of a slope rather than at the top — water runs downhill, and so a hilltop pond looks out of place. If you intend to grow water-lilies, be sure to choose a sunny location.

Before beginning to dig the hole for your fiberglass pool, decide where you will stockpile the removed soil — there is going to be a lot of it. Lay the unit on the ground, trace around it using a metal tool such as a shovel, pick or trowel, then dig the hole slightly deeper (6 inches to 1 foot) than is needed to hold the fiberglass pool liner. This additional space allows you to finish off the bottom with a layer of sand approximately 4 inches thick. The sand acts to cushion the liner (whether fiberglass or flexible membrane) against roots and stones that might puncture or otherwise damage it. Besides, it is easier to backfill a hole with sand than to dig more dirt out later. Excavate the soil, removing any rocks or tree roots.

Although they're a bit more difficult to install than fiberglass pools, flexible-membrane liners allow you to design a pond or wetland garden in any size or shape you choose.

A Before digging, mark the outline of your wetland garden with a long rope and stakes or a garden hose.

B Begin digging at the center, working toward the edges. You may want to construct a shallow ledge around the perimeter for emergent plants.

C Lay the liner in the sun for half an hour to soften it. Then carefully place it into the excavation, smoothing out creases as you go.

D Fill the pool with water. When it is nearly full, trim back excess material from the edges.

E Cover the edges of the liner with sod or rocks.

Install the pool at grade or only slightly higher than the surrounding soil to keep debris from washing in, but never below the level of the surrounding soil. After placing the fiberglass pool liner carefully in the excavated hole, lay a 2- by 4-inch board — long enough to extend from side-to-side — across the top as a support for a carpenter's level. Check both lengthwise and crosswise to be sure the pool is level. Once it is in place and level, begin to fill it with water while back-filling around the sides with some of the stockpiled soil to insure that the fit is snug.

Any overhanging edge can be hidden with rocks. Make sure they are installed securely enough to bear a person's weight since someone, child or adult, is sure to stand on them. You can also conceal the edges with plants, or an artfully placed log. In fact, a combination of these edge-masking techniques will create the most natural appearance.

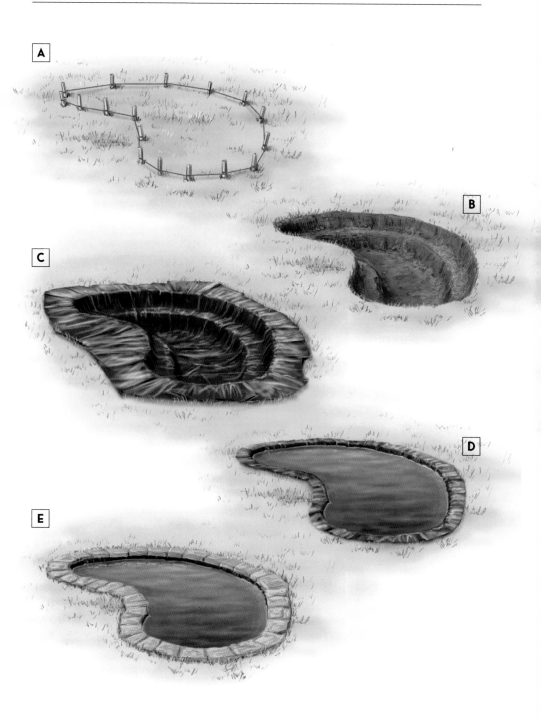

The edges of this pool were masked with flat rocks. Make sure any rocks are installed securely enough to bear a person's weight because someone, child or adult, is sure to stand on them.

FLEXIBLE LINERS

Although a bit more difficult to install, flexible-membrane pond liners allow you to design a pond or wetland garden in the precise size, shape and depth you choose. Do *not* use left-over swimming pool liners. They contain anti-algae chemicals that are harmful to plants and fish. The liner must be fish-grade plastic. EPDM is long-wearing and resistant to UV degradation. Butyl rubber liners are another choice. While thinner membranes are less expensive, 45 mil liners, which have a life of twenty years, are well worth the additional cost.

Most home gardeners make their membrane-lined pools 14 to 24 inches deep. The liners are available in pre-cut sections in sizes ranging from 5 by 5 feet up to 30 by 30 feet, or by the roll in widths ranging from 5 to 30 feet in 5-foot increments, and 50 or 100 feet long. If you need something even larger, you can piece together lengths using special, double-sided, 3-inch-wide tape designed for just that purpose. Before you join them, cover the edges of the plastic for added strength with 6-inch-wide patching tape, available where liners are sold. While this adds to the initial cost of the project, in the long run it is more economical to seal your pool

To keep your pool clean, you'll need either fish or a mechanical water filtration and purification system, such as the one being installed here. Mechanical filters need to be cleaned as often as once a week, depending on conditions.

well from the start. Otherwise, you may later find yourself having to remove plants and catch and hold fish while you drain the pool, repair and refill it.

It's worth repeating that when deciding where to place your pool, you should consider visibility and choose a level site away from trees — in autumn their leaves will collect in the pool and foul the water.

To figure out the size of the liner, you'll need to record the longest and widest points of your pool. Then decide on the depth. If it will be 18 inches deep, add 4 feet to the length and width of the rectangle's dimensions. For each additional 6-inch depth, add another 12 inches to both the width and length. If you've never before installed a flexible-membrane liner, you might want to add another 12 inches to the length and the width as a fudge factor for errors.

Get together a group of friends to help with the digging, soil moving and placement of the liner. Unfortunately, there is no simple formula for figuring the number of friends you'll need. Approximate the outline of your pond with a long rope or garden hose, stepping back and making any adjustments to the shape now, in the planning stage, rather than after you have begun the excavation. Use a half-moon edger or sharp shovel to mark the perimeter. Or if you prefer, remove a thin strip of sod to clearly indicate the outline.

Begin digging from the center, working towards the edges. Check to make sure the bottom of the excavation is level, as suggested for the fiberglass pool. Remove any protruding rocks and roots. When you're digging and shaping the excavation, consider constructing a shallow ledge or lip around the perimeter. This will allow you to grow shallow water, emergent plants such as arrow arum and pickerel rush, which want only a few inches of water over their roots.

Since flexible liners can tear or puncture, you may want to install a geotextile between the soil and the liner, which, like a carpet underpad, protects the liner. It should be positioned in the excavation first, with the liner installed on top of it. Water-garden nurseries sell the geotextile separately or bonded to the liner. If you decide to use the bonded version, be aware that it cannot be seamed to another piece. The bonded liner is also stiff, making it harder to place. However, you don't need to worry about the liner and the geotextile shifting relative to one another — a particular problem with irregular shapes — as you do when the two pieces are separate. To reduce costs, some water gardeners use old jute or other fiber carpet pads instead of geotextiles.

If possible, lay the liner in the sun to warm up thirty minutes or so before you actually install it. The stronger the sun (depending on time of year and day), the more rapidly the liner will soften. Do this on the driveway, as heat build-up under the liner will kill plants or lawn. It takes two or more people to handle liners with the care necessary to avoid damage. Besides, they're heavy — a 100-square-foot piece of 45 mil liner weighs 29 pounds. Carefully place the liner into the excavation and unfold it, smoothing out folds and creases as you go. Because you will be standing on the liner, wear rubber boots or soft-soled shoes to protect it.

Now you can begin filling the pool with water. When the pool is nearly full, trim back any excess material at the edge. If you do it too soon, the weight of the water may leave a skimpier edge than you would like as it snugs the liner to the sides of the excavation. Pin the edging flap to the soil with 4- to 6-inch-long #10 nails. As with fiberglass pools, the edge can be covered with flat-bottomed rocks, or you can even roll the sod back into place over it.

OTHER MATERIALS

Concrete and bentonite clay are two other materials used to keep water in a wetland garden. Although they are durable, installing them is probably beyond the capabilities of most homeowners. Concrete has the advantage of being flexible when first mixed and strong when cured. The difficulties arise from its tendency

For a self-contained pool with no connection to a natural waterway (hence no means for the fish to swim away), exotic fish such as colorful koi are an option.

to crack unless installed absolutely correctly. And concrete pools that develop a leak seem determined to do so in perpetuity. Since concrete will flow when wet, any vertical side needs to be contained within a wooden form until it sets. Concrete is best installed with a reinforcing wire to provide additional support. For large pools, rebar may be necessary. New concrete must be treated to remove chemicals harmful to fish and plants. Unless there is a mason in your family, I'd leave concrete pools to the professionals.

Like concrete, bentonite clay also requires special handling. And unless the clay is locally available, shipping costs significantly add to the overall expense. When properly installed and tamped with a vibrator to form a water-tight seal, it can be used to line large ponds. Where it works well, bentonite clay is fabulous, but if the water level sinks and the clay dries, it will leak. If muskrats tunnel into the sides, it will leak. If plants root into the bentonite clay, it will also leak.

A BALANCED ECOSYSTEM

Wetland gardens require a healthy mix of plants in order to be self-sustaining. As well as the water-lilies that exemplify water gardens to most people, and the emergent plants that naturally fringe the edges of a pond, balanced wetlands need submergent plants. Most of their growth never reaches the surface. However, they take up nutrients dissolved in the water, remove carbon dioxide, add oxygen and provide mats where mature fish can lay their eggs and young fish can hide. By utilizing nutrients that would otherwise support algal growth, submergent plants help prevent algae blooms that spoil a pond's appearance. But keep in mind that a pond is not supposed to be crystal clear; if you can still see your hand when it is submerged 5 or 6 inches below the surface, that's fine.

A balanced pool also needs fish to filter the water. Besides, they add to your enjoyment of a water garden, much as butterflies and birds enhance a flower garden. And they eat mosquito larvae, keeping your pond free of these pests. For a self-contained pool with no connection to a natural watercourse (hence no means for the fish to swim away), exotic, non-native fish such as goldfish, golden orfe or koi are an attractive option. Gambusia, also called mosquito fish, or even guppies from your local pet store may be used in a container water garden or half-whiskey barrel. If you are enhancing a natural pond, native fish probably are already present.

The alternative to fish is mechanical water filtration and water purification (which also may be necessary if the pool is relatively small and you decide to keep koi; though attractive and responsive to humans, they root around the bottom, stirring up the muck and clouding the water). Electricity and water are a hazardous combination, so be sure to have a licensed electrician install a ground-fault interrupter circuit. The size of the pump will depend on the size of your pool. Filters can be mechanical or biological. Mechanical filters need to be cleaned periodically — as often as once a week, depending on conditions. Biological filters utilize gravel to filter and nitrifying bacteria to digest debris.

While it may not be quite as simple as "just add water," water gardening is not difficult. Creating a water garden for a patio, deck or terrace can be as easy as planting a pot of petunias. Start small, for like any other kind of garden you'll learn as you go. Proof positive: Most of the water gardeners I know have more than one pool.

Planting & Maintaining Backyard Wetlands

BY FRED ROZUMALSKI

THE COMBINATION OF SUN, moisture and rich organic soils makes wetlands among the most productive, dynamic and fascinating plant communities in North America. Yet planting and maintaining a wetland or a lake edge on your property presents a unique set of landscape problems. Whether you are re-creating or restoring a freshwater wetland, understanding how these areas function — their fluctuating water levels, vegetation cycles and vegetation zones — will make caring for them simpler than you may think and well worth the effort.

ZONE AESTHETICS

Wetland vegetation grows in visually distinct zones or bands. These zones usually are each dominated by one or two species. Many subdominant wetland plants thrive in more than one zone or straddle zones. The heights and shapes of the dominant species determine the character of the zone (see "Wetland Zones," page 11). In some cases, the dominant plants are coarsely textured or bold in character. In other cases, the dominant species are finely textured reeds and grasses.

In all wetlands, the composition of species progressively changes, beginning

Wet meadow zones are areas of natural filtration and should never be cleared.

This pond's wet meadow zone was converted to lawn but is being restored.

at the shallow outer edge where the wetland meets the upland, and ending at the center of the wetland, where the water is deepest. This progression of species is related to the depth of water and the duration of flooding. Water level is never constant in a wetland. In the spring, it is high and then dries down. It may rise again after a summer storm. Plants survive because they are able to tolerate flooding and because during dry-down periods, the organic soils stay moist due to capillary action from the deeper zones — the natural tendancy of water to move to an area of less saturation.

There is no absolute rule as to how long flooding lasts, but generally the wet meadow zone is flooded from two to five weeks in spring. The emergent zone typically dries down for a short time in mid-summer. The deep marsh dries down only during drought years.

In home landscapes, people often clear away the wet meadow zone — the area that reaches inland from the edge of a lake or pond and contains saturated soil — to extend their lawns. However, this is part of a natural buffer zone, an area of natural filtration that extends from the upland down to the seasonal high-water level. This buffer filters out eroded soil and other particulate matter that can blow in or wash down from upland areas, and is best left intact. If it has been converted to lawn, it should be restored to its natural state.

DESIGN

When you begin planning to restore a wetland, aim to mimic the zones and plant the species found in nature — those that would have grown on your site before it was altered. Look to undisturbed wetlands or lake shores in your area as a "template" for species that grow under similar conditions. Observe the overall pattern of zones, how species are grouped according to water depth. Note the types of species growing and how closely and evenly they are dispersed. Take notes and photographs to aid your memory.

First, consider the emergent zone, which is in the water closest to the land's edge, where plants "emerge" from the water. Because it supports relatively few plant species, including arrowhead, pickerel weed and hard-stem bulrush, which grow in large colonies and in broad patterns, this zone is relatively simple to design. Do not plan to plant these species as densely as you see them growing in natural stands because they spread quickly. Plan to establish four or five species in large clusters. As they grow and seed, they will thicken and gradually move to other areas where they are best suited.

Next, consider the design of the wetland edge or wet meadow zone, which floods briefly in the spring and after summer storms and remains saturated during most of the year. Because it abuts the rest of the yard, it is the zone over which most gardeners wish to exert the most control. Although many plants grow here, the wet meadow zone is typically dominated by just a few species of grasses or sedges. In your design, plan to establish plants in clusters across the entire buffer zone, with approximately 3 feet between them to allow for spread. Plant wildflowers at the same 3-foot intervals as the sedges, so that in the final design scheme plants will be spaced about 1-1/2 feet apart. If there is a potential for erosion, space plants 1 foot apart.

ON-SITE DESIGN

After you do the initial planning of the numbers and species of plants you want to grow and acquire them from specialized nurseries (see "Nursery Sources," page 104), you can begin the on-site design. First, lay out the grasses and sedges in a large grid directly on the ground with approximately 3 feet between individual plants. Group dominant species in large colonies as you observed them in nature.

The multiple vertical stems of the grasses and sedges are the visual element that holds the design together. Add wildflowers to achieve as much show of color as you desire.

Your close observation of natural areas will pay off when you begin deciding on the placement of wildflowers in the meadow zone. Some species, including blue flag iris, turtlehead and sweet flag, grow best on the wetter end of the planting bed along the water's edge. Others, such as redstem aster, naturally occur slightly uphill in somewhat drier soil. Place each plant in the type of soil and setting where it's typically found. To place wildflowers within the matrix of grasses and sedges, refer back to your photographs or mental images of the way you saw them growing in the wild — either individually or in large groups.

VEGETATION CYCLING

Wetland vegetation continually changes both in response to seasonal flooding and dry spells and to very dry and wet years (see "Wetland Ecology for Gardeners," page 7). Learning how to restore or enhance wetlands requires close observation of the vegetation cycle that accompanies these moisture fluctuations. During drought years, water levels drop, exposing wetland soils. Exposed to full sun, these moist, organic soils provide ideal conditions for seed — often dropped years before and stored in the mud — to sprout. As the drought ends and water levels rise, the seedlings grow rapidly. And so, before planting, you must re-create this "mudflat" condition — removing debris and any invasive plants like hybrid cattail and purple loosestrife. The seeds of most species require open soil and will not germinate below water.

In wetlands there is also a natural progression of species establishment. Early colonizing species like smartweed and beggar's tick dominate first. They protect the seedlings of species that are slower to establish.

PLANTING

If you're restoring a wetland over an acre in size, it is most economical to plant seed. Seed should be purchased locally or collected from nearby wetlands with permission. Seedlings of hard-to-find or showy species can be planted as you seed and will provide a more immediate visual impact. A cover crop of an annual plant such as oats will prevent soil erosion in all planted areas.

Some species, particularly sedges, do not establish well from seed. In order to

Locate plants in the type of soil and setting in which they naturally occur. Blue flag iris thrives in the emergent zone along the water's edge.

The seeds of most species won't germinate below water. Before planting, you must re-create the natural mudflat condition that occurs during droughts.

achieve a good diversity, you'll have to plant late-cycle species such as sedges and lilies as nursery-grown stock during the second or third year after the initial seeding to ensure their establishment. In zones with standing water, you'll also need to use live plants or root stocks because the seeds of most species will not germinate under water. In areas dominated by invasive species or where native species are scarce, plants again are a better choice than seed because they establish quickly and are less likely to be carried away by wind or water.

In areas where at least some native vegetation remains, reintroducing plants or seed may not be necessary as any propagules in the seed bank will probably germinate, given the right growing conditions. Where the wet meadow zone has been replaced by turfgrasses, simply removing the lawn may enable seed-bank species to regenerate or nearby plants to seed in. After removing turf, preferably by smothering it with plastic or some other material, seed in an annual crop like oats to prevent erosion while native species establish.

Optimal planting time varies by region. In the North, it is best to plant in late spring, after the water recedes. West of the Rockies, the best time to plant is in the fall. In the southern states fall and winter are best. But it's always a good idea to check with a regional nursery because wetland conditions vary, even within regions.

Before planting, you must eradicate any existing invasive plant species. Chemical herbicides should only be used as a last resort. Begin by trying to remove the invasives mechanically — either pulling weeds by hand or with a weeding tool. (See the Brooklyn Botanic Garden handbook *Invasive Plants* for more information on the best controls for specific invasive weeds.) When herbicides are necessary, a glyphosate formulation such as Rodeo, available at most nurseries, is the best choice because it can be used in areas near open water. More tenacious invasives may require several applications over an extended period. Once it is dead, remove the unwanted vegetation by either raking it away or cutting it back.

Next, plant seedlings and sow seed directly into the soil. No soil amendments are necessary. Tilling is required only in areas that will be seeded.

MAINTAINING YOUR WETLAND

Traditional landscape maintenance techniques can cause havoc in a wetland environment. Many of us do not realize the great damage we do to wetlands until it is too late. Mowing edges destroys wildlife habitat, kills interesting plants and eliminates the buffer that is essential for preserving water quality. Mismanage a wetland or lake edge and you can cause algal blooms and fish kills and encourage the growth of invasive species. Continued removal of invasive plant species such as reed canary grass, purple loosestrife and hybrid cattail is an important part of wetland garden maintenance. Keep an eye out for invasives and take action as soon as possible to prevent serious infestations.

Just as important as the management of invasive species is the proper management of the upland — that is, the rest of your yard. Wetland and lake quality are directly influenced by the stormwater they receive. If the stormwater runoff contains silt, pesticides and fertilizers, your wetland or lake will suffer. One thing that will help is reducing the size of your lawn and replacing it with native vegetation such as wildflowers or shrub thickets. On the remaining lawn, reduce fertilizer use. Instead of synthetic petrochemical-based fertilizers, use less soluble organic brands that less readily wash away in runoff. Plant a buffer zone at the edge of your lake or wetland. A swath of native species, preferably over 25 feet wide uphill from the normal water line, will filter the runoff, create habitat for wildlife — and, as a bonus, provide you with a beautiful and a low maintenance wildflower garden.

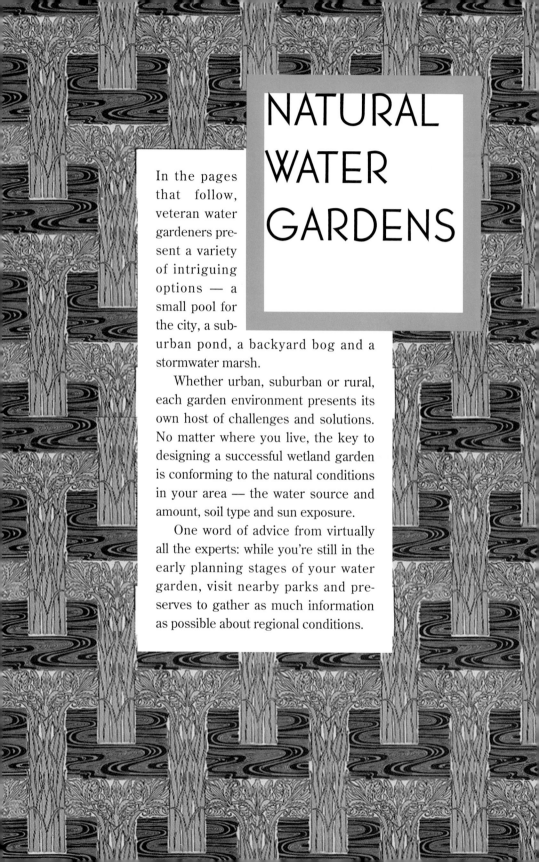

NATURAL WATER GARDENS

In the pages that follow, veteran water gardeners present a variety of intriguing options — a small pool for the city, a suburban pond, a backyard bog and a stormwater marsh.

Whether urban, suburban or rural, each garden environment presents its own host of challenges and solutions. No matter where you live, the key to designing a successful wetland garden is conforming to the natural conditions in your area — the water source and amount, soil type and sun exposure.

One word of advice from virtually all the experts: while you're still in the early planning stages of your water garden, visit nearby parks and preserves to gather as much information as possible about regional conditions.

Pools & Ponds

BY CAROL FRANKLIN

ALTHOUGH DIFFERENT IN size and location, the pool and pond described in this chapter are both ecologically balanced systems containing interdependent communities of aquatic plants, animals, insects and microorganisms. The pool designed for a tiny, primarily paved backyard in downtown Philadelphia, Pennsylvania, demonstrates that a balanced-ecosystem pool can be created even in the smallest of urban gardens where much of the natural expression of water has been eliminated. A large residential property in Greenwich, Connecticut, gave us the opportunity to create a pond with qualities similar to those found in northeastern forests. Its generous size — over a third of an acre — its naturally landscaped site and its connection to the regional water system enable this pond to function as a living system and made it possible for us to organize the plants in naturally occurring patterns.

As is the case with any kind of ecosystem, no two water gardens are alike. Designing your pool or pond in keeping with its surroundings — whether urban, suburban or rural — will lead to its own delightful surprises and creative solutions.

AN URBAN POOL

Since a pool is a living system, it brings a new, ever-evolving series of relationships to the garden. The 6- by 10-foot pool is this Philadelphia garden's centerpiece, enlivening and enriching the space. By attracting attention downward into

36

the water, a small pool adds a dimension of depth and an element of mystery. In this urban backyard the aquatic plants are the main flower garden. The water not only hosts its own wildlife but attracts an array of visiting creatures — birds, insects and small mammals — that come to drink and bathe.

CONSTRUCTION

Because the only access to the garden is through an alleyway too narrow for a truck to enter, a cast-concrete pool was out of the question. Instead, we built the pool using liquid concrete sprayed from a long hose onto a cage of steel-mesh reinforcing shaped to the pool's contours. A series of planting pockets comprising a simplified version of wetland plant zones was built into the walls, allowing plants to be placed at the appropriate water depths.

A 6- by 10-foot pool is this Philadelphia garden's centerpiece. The pool's aquatic plants are the main flower garden in the urban backyard.

Since the garden is located in Philadelphia where freezes and thaws are common in winter, the pool's edge was made from a beam strong enough to resist the pressure of ice. (In warmer climes, extra reinforcement may not be necessary.) At four feet, the pool was deep enough to both prevent frost heaving and enable the fish to take refuge below the ice in the winter.

Nothing destroys the magic of a sunken pool more readily than seeing the edge of the container. The single most frequent mistake in pool building is poor edge construction — visible concrete, an even line of stones or bits of liner peeking through. In order for the water to meet rock rather than concrete, the edge of a professionally constructed concrete pool should be sturdy enough to support large paving stones and boulders overhanging the water.

Planting pockets built into the pool's walls create a simplified version of wetland zones for native emergent plants like arrowheads and pickerel weed.

PLANTING AND MANAGEMENT

Before we planted this pool, it was filled and emptied several times over a period of three to four weeks to remove excess alkali on the concrete's surface. If this chore is too onerous, products that neutralize calcium and lime are available from pond-supply catalogs.

Next, we filled the planting pockets with a good sandy loam, rich in organic matter. A pool filled with city tapwater does not require additional fertilizer because the water contains nutrients.

All the anchored emergents — arrowheads, blue water iris and pickerel weed, as well as those with floating leaves such as spatterdocks and water-lilies — were planted before the pool was filled. In this small pool, fully grown, two-year plants in containers, with well developed heads and root systems, provided an instant visual effect. Only hardy, regionally native plants that can survive the Philadelphia climate were selected.

After planting, the pond was filled with water, slowly enough to allow the water to gradually seep in and saturate the soil. A layer of gravel was placed over the soil in the plant pockets to prevent muddying of the water. When the pond was full, the submerged aquatics — coontail, waterweed and water celery — were dropped into the water in small bunches weighted with stones, so that they would sink to the bottom.

After a month or two, when the plants were established, we added fish, snails, insects and microorganisms which are commercially available from pond-supply catalogs. Waiting allowed the chlorine in the tapwater to volatilize, eliminating the need for additional dechlorinization chemicals.

For a balanced system in which all of the species in the pool are functioning interdependently, only a few fish should be added. As they multiply, the extra animals need to be removed as they overburden the pool with waste. This pool was stocked with koi, showy, bright orange-red fish. Small indigenous fish would have created an entirely native ecosystem. However, they are drab in color and shy in temperament.

After it was planted and stocked and the chlorine from the tapwater had dissipated, the pool was "inoculated" with a gallon of water taken from a natural pond — a practice which ideally should be repeated every two to

A gallon of natural pond water is added to this urban pool every few years to maintain populations of organisms that keep the ecosystem healthy.

three years to maintain the system's health. Natural pondwater is rich in bacteria, microscopic plants and water insects, which make the system more complex biologically. Bacteria and snails, important but often overlooked members of this ecosystem, play a critical role in keeping the water clean. They are also available from pond-supply catalogs.

Healthy water in a balanced-life pool is like good beer — clear, pale brown and well aged! A new pool may go through several rapid changes when first established. Algae growth can turn the water bright green, particularly if there is ample sunlight and the pond has been filled with city tapwater, often rich in nitrogen and phosphorus. If this happens, the best strategy is to wait. Eventually, the nutrients that fueled the bloom will be used up and a natural balance created. Pools that turn green should never be emptied and refilled because the algae bloom will only begin again. In order for a pool to become a mini-ecosystem, the water, plants and animals in it should be left to develop over the years.

This pond in suburban Connecticut was edged with burlap to keep soil from washing away. Holes were cut in the burlap to place the plants.

The rhizomes of floating plants, such as water-lilies, were planted in tubs of soil, weighted with stones and sunk into the water.

Most pools settle down after the first season and become largely self-sustaining. Still, a few small management tasks are required. The water level in a small pool should be topped off when low. In this pool rainwater, which is chlorine-free, is used as an alternative to tapwater; it's captured in a barrel from roof run-off. However the rainwater is also full of nutrients such as nitrogen from automobile exhaust and factory emissions and may cause temporary algae blooms.

Over time this pool, like all healthy balanced pools, developed a dark organic layer on the bottom, formed by slowly rotting leaves and other organic debris. As this layer will gradually fill in a small system, it should be removed every year or so in the fall, depending on how many trees are nearby and how dirty the water is. The simplest method is to use a net made to skim swimming pools.

Mechanical pool skimmers will keep the surface free of debris. They are available commercially. If you choose, you can also do this job by hand.

In the winter, if the pool is completely covered with ice, carbon dioxide and methane released by decaying organic matter can build up. To allow the fish to breathe, *gently* make an opening in the ice — smashing it will give them a concussion!

A FOREST POND WITH WETLANDS

The pond in Connecticut is nestled between three dramatic outcrops of granite in a rocky dell. A waterfall cascades over the front face of the central rock outcrop

The pond is nestled between three dramatic outcrops of granite in a rocky dell. After debris had been removed from the site, a heavy plastic liner was placed in the excavation and tucked into a groove in the rocks. A manmade waterfall cascades over the front face of one outcrop and into the pond.

and into the pond. The dell had been used as a dump for garden refuse. Although unsightly and highly degraded, it was an officially designated wetland. Therefore, the Town of Greenwich required a permit before construction, stipulating that the existing wetlands be replaced. When finished, this pond not only met those requirements but provided a fringe of newly created wetlands and ephemeral pools that doubled the size of the original wetlands, and provided a variety of lowland landscapes with greater species diversity than existed before.

CONSTRUCTION

When the pond was excavated, all the removed muck — the decayed material — was stored and gradually reused both on site and in other gardens. We placed a six-inch layer of gravel on the excavated bottom to level the surface and protect the pond liner from sharp rocks. A soft polyethylene fabric placed on top of the gravel provided a second level of protection. Professional installers then laid down a heavy vinyl liner in large sections which were joined together and sealed. The liner was weighed down and held in place with a layer of stones.

To ensure that groundwater cannot push up the liner from underneath, we laid a network of perforated pipes in the gravel to collect any water and carry it to a sump just beyond the pond's edge. From there, it is pumped back into the pond. At several outlet points, excess water overflows the pond's edge and runs into the surrounding wetlands, where it seeps back into the groundwater.

We used this system to fill the pond when it was built and it continues to operate, topping off the water level when it lowers during seasonal dry spells. It also helps move water through the pond, providing a means of flushing. Almost all the water is recycled. The only water loss is from evaporation, which is minimal in this shady, wooded location.

To create the natural illusion of rocky outcrops plunging into the water, we undercut the rockface at the waterline using jackhammers. The plastic liner was tucked into a groove in the rock. Boulders from the site were carefully placed on top of the liner, giving the appearance that the rock continues down into the pond. To create the waterfall, which helps to ensure adequate oxygenation of the pond, a small, separate recirculating water system was installed to pump water up from the pond; it flows out of a copper pipe we inserted through a small hole drilled up through the outcrop.

PLANTING AND MANAGEMENT

Special stone plant pockets were built into the south-facing side of the pond and filled with the rich organic excavated muck. Because a large pond takes time to fill — up to several weeks, depending on the water source — and the aquatic plants would have dried out without sufficient water, the pond was planted after filling.

We used dormant rootstocks, plugs and bareroot plants because they are easy to handle and relatively inexpensive. Different planting methods were used for each zone. The corms and tubers of emergents like the arrowheads were wrapped in small burlap bags, weighted with stones and pressed into the muck in the same way that rice seedlings are planted in a paddy field. The rhizomes of floating emergents, such as water-lilies, were planted in tubs of soil, weighted with stones and sunk into the water to a depth of three feet. We simply threw the submerged oxygenators, which come bare root, into the pond. Container-grown rushes, sedges and ferns were planted like perennials on the dike that separates the pond from the wetlands. The soil here was covered with burlap to prevent it from washing away and holes were cut in the burlap to place the plants. After the plants were established, we added native fish — bass, pickerel and sunnies.

This pond responds to the seasons, flooding into the adjacent wetlands and lowland forest in wet weather and shrinking during dry periods. Allowing a pond to draw down a foot or two promotes plant growth. Because the pond is lined and sufficiently deep, there's always some water to sustain the aquatic ecosystem.

A Stormwater Marsh

BY CRAIG TUFTS

DID YOU EVER STOP to think about how much water rolls off your roof each year? If you live in Tucson, the quantity might be small. Where I live, though, in suburban northern Virginia, summer thunderstorms and winter snows drop 40 inches of precipitation annually. This stormwater rolls down driveways and over roads, collecting motor oil, cigarettes, pesticides and pet wastes from street gutters as it flows towards small streams where, over a period of years, it causes extensive environmental damage.

According to some minor calculations, I figured that just half of the runoff from my roof could supply me with 14,000 gallons of water a year. I reasoned that rather than letting the rain continue to wash unused across lawn and into a nearby stream, I could use that water in a more productive way. Such a large quantity could fill a big fish tank or moisten a nifty little marsh, for example. Since childhood I've liked the moisture-loving plants that grow in marshes — cardinal flower, common rush, great blue lobelia. Many of these would thrive in regular soil as well, but I wanted to establish a plant community, an ecosystem, rather than simply design a formal landscape.

WHAT'S A MARSH?

A naturally occurring marsh is a wetland characterized by predominantly herbaceous sun-loving plants, some shrubs and, for at least part of the year, standing water. In time, as shrubs and sedges are replaced by trees, a marsh eventually

The steady source of water from the nearby roof made this a good site for a marsh. It is also on the south side of the house, a perfect location for sun-loving marsh plants.

becomes a swamp (a wetland dominated by trees). However, by controlling the water and with judicious weeding, a marsh can be made to retain its character and will continue to host a variety of herbaceous plants.

BUILDING A MARSH

I chose the site for my marsh based on access to water from the roof of my house, which fortunately was close to a site flat enough to accommodate a marsh. Although you could use a driveway or other surface to supply stormwater runoff, a roof is ideal both because gravity works in your favor to bring water to your marsh and because the water quality tends to be good. The only potentially polluting nutrients my roof may contribute are some bird droppings.

To grow the types of plants I wanted I needed a sunny location, so I chose the south side of my house. A third consideration was soil quality. Very sandy soil is too permeable to adequately hold water. Luckily, I had a good deal of absorbant clay in my soil.

As with any project involving significant landscape change, I needed to consult my local homeowner's association and municipal government to make sure the intended marsh was permissible before I began excavating.

My marsh project began to take shape eight years ago in early winter. Step one was to outline the perimeter of the proposed site. My marsh, about 20 by 30 feet, is irregular in outline, due more to encounters with bedrock than to my sense of design. Using a small rototiller, spading fork and a digging bar to wedge the rocks out of the ground, I stripped the sod from my outlined area, then excavated the subsoil and rock to about 14 inches deep, allowing for an emergency spillway, an area of turfgrass at the lower end of the marsh; during heavy rains, the water can collect here without causing erosion. As I excavated, I used levels supported on two-by-fours to make sure that the ground was even.

Next, I connected a length of flexible plastic pipe to a downspout from my roof, angling it away from the house and burying it beneath the ground and into the marsh. However, during the next rainstorm, when the water backed up inside the pipe, I discovered I needed to increase the overall angle by 4 inches. What's more, because I had used perforated pipe — simply because it had been lying around — I found that too much water was leaking out en route to the marsh and flowing back towards the foundation of the house. I tried using clay to seal the soil surface around the pipe, but that proved ineffective. So, in April, I replaced the perforated pipe with a solid piece and re-excavated the ditch at a greater angle, thus stopping what had become an overactive sump pump in my basement.

Plants for the marsh garden were selected because they are colorful and also because they provide nectar for butterflies, hummingbirds and other pollinators.

MARSH PLANTS

Because my soil had the same consistency as construction debris — clay and rock fragment — I worked sand, a dozen buckets of compost, a good quantity of the original subsoil and leaf mold into the top few inches of soil. Using my tough little rototiller, I mixed the marsh soil in place. I mimicked a vegetation zone pattern by simply varying the original basin depth, then backfilling uniformly with my marsh soil.

The last and most enjoyable task was plant selection. My choices weren't only based on plant size, fragrance, hardiness, color and seasonal interest. Because I was determined that my marsh attract butterflies and hummingbirds, I factored in their needs for nectar and chose other plants that provide food for their caterpillars.

I planted Joe-pye weed to attract butterflies, cardinal flowers for hummingbirds and great blue lobelia for bumblebees. Some of the woody plants, especially buttonbush and sweet pepperbush, attract butterflies as well as other pollinators. Some of these insects are excellent biological pest-control agents, too.

Eventually, this mass of herbaceous plants and shrubs provided nesting areas for birds, including cardinals, song sparrows, catbirds and common yellowthroats. Although I wasn't intending to attract mammals — deer, raccoons and squirrels hardly need an incentive — small species do use the marsh as a place to hide and forage for the plants' fruit.

Plant placement was largely determined by my desire to create a screen from my neighbor's house on the upslope of the marsh and by the plants' water requirements. Because the roots of spicebush have to remain fairly wet, it went into a relatively deep area of the marsh, near the water's entry point. Sweet pepperbush needs less water, so I placed it in a drier section.

I look forward to the day when spicebush, sweet pepperbush, buttonbush, silky dogwood and wafer ash will tower over the cardinal flower, monkey flower, swamp milkweed, turtlehead and pickerel weed. Joe-pye weed now looms over the downstream end of the marsh, providing a transition between the marsh, which supports many pollinator species, and the garden specifically designed as a nectar feast for butterflies. Eight years after its creation, my marsh supports about forty-five plant species.

Buttonbush attracts butterflies as well as other pollinators.

Great blue lobelia is an excellent choice for bumblebees.

Although the marsh was planted primarily for pollinators, other guests show up as well.

Hummingbirds are attracted to the bright red blooms of the cardinal flower.

MARSH MAINTENANCE

For the most part, I've let nature take its course and done little in the way of maintaining my marsh. A two- or three-inch rainfall may result in standing water for a day before it's absorbed into the ground. And once, during a severe summer drought lasting more than three weeks, I did add graywater pumped from my washing machine. After concluding that I didn't like the look of that and wasn't too comfortable with the types of nutrients I was potentially adding to the soil, I did draw on some city water for a couple of days as the drought continued.

Although marsh gardens are largely restricted to regions with fairly good rainfall such as the Northeast, Southeast and Northwest, if you live in a drier area your yard could potentially support a marsh as well, provided you line the excavation with a plastic liner (see "Constructing a Wetland Garden," page 19). A number of municipal and county governments around the country are promoting "rain" gardens as a way to lessen sudden surges into local streams. Certain areas, including Prince George's County, Maryland, and the Portland, Oregon, metropolitan area, are educating construction engineers to establish areas in new developments where stormwater can collect, sit and then slowly percolate into the ground.

Some day, I'll live next to a natural marsh. Meanwhile, I'm enjoying the added dimension that my homemade mini-marsh has brought — the butterflies, birds, amphibians and moisture-loving plants.

A Bog Garden

BY C. COLSTON BURRELL

FEW GARDENERS ARE LUCKY ENOUGH to possess a moist spot, much less a true bog. I garden in Minneapolis on a dry terrace adjacent to the Mississippi River, in silty loam above limestone bedrock. For an ardent plant collector such as myself, lack of moist soil is a cruel fate. I love turtleheads, sedges, skunk cabbage and iris, plants of low woods and wet meadows which demand continuous moisture to thrive. In my dry, silty soil, it seemed impossible to even think of growing them. Impossible, that is, until I thought of creating an artificial bog garden.

Natural bogs form in glacial lake beds and shallow depressions over hundreds of years. My challenge was to create a consistently moist soil environment for plants on a flat, well-drained river terrace. Employing the same technology available to water gardeners who build artificial ponds, I used a plastic-lined trench. But instead of filling the liner with water, I filled it with soil. Unlike a true marsh, which has open water, my bog provides a haven for plants that like wet feet; there is no standing water.

Keeping the soil moist was not the only consideration in the making of my bog. The relationship of the new bog garden to the overall landscape design was also paramount — I didn't want the bog garden to look like a botanical freak show. My garden is laid out formally. A rectangular lawn and terrace form a long axis, flanked on both sides by eight-foot-deep beds. The bog garden had to com-

In nature, a bog contains plants uniquely adapted to wet, acidic soils. In an artificial bog, you can choose from a variety of moisture-loving perennials, bulbs and shrubs such as the ferns and ligularia above.

plement and maintain the integrity of this design framework, forming an exuberant planting bed with lots of relaxed and tumbling plants to mirror the one on the opposite side of the lawn. I decided to run the bog garden for 25 feet along the entire length of the lawn. On either end, it blends imperceptibly into the existing beds, creating a visually unified whole. Though the lines of the garden are rectilinear and formal, the overall effect is relaxed and comfortable. The velvety lawn is surrounded on all sides by lush plantings. The bog garden fits in perfectly.

BUILDING A BOG GARDEN

Once the size and shape of the new bog were designed, the most challenging task was excavating the hole. I decided to make the bog two feet deep. In retrospect, I should have dug down to three, allowing the dictates of the plants to determine the bog's depth rather than my physical stamina. Since small excavations dry out quickly, the larger you make your bog garden, the better. Deeper soil is more accommodating to the root systems of mature plants. In other words, if you are thinking about designing several small bog gardens, you would be better off with one large one at least 2-1/2 feet deep.

Start digging at one end of the trench, moving down its length.

Starting at one end, I dug the trench to its full depth as I moved down its length. While digging, I kept the walls sloped outward slightly from the bottom of the trench to keep them from caving in. To protect the lawn, I piled the soil on a tarp. The mountain of soil that grew next to the pit caused quite a stir on the block. Neighbors appeared from all corners to investigate. The 8-foot prairie plants I had used in the front garden had made them suspicious. But when they heard I was building a bog, they thought I had really lost it. Now that the hole is filled and the plants are in place, they can't even tell that the bog is there.

After excavating, I lined the trench by rolling out an 8 mm plastic sheet. The use of a single, unbroken sheet is important because the seams created by using several overlapping sheets will not hold water.

Some drainage is necessary to keep the crowns of the plants (the point where the roots meet the top growth) from rotting. Because I garden in USDA zone 4, where winter temperatures reach -30 degrees F, I was also concerned about the cold. I didn't want water and ice to come into contact with the crowns, so I placed drainage holes around the periphery of the liner, a foot below the soil surface. By duplicating the conditions under which many plants grow in the wild, I ensured that the top of the soil — where the crowns are — remains relatively dry, while the roots are kept moist.

After unrolling the plastic sheet and centering it over the trench, I let it settle in, checking to make sure that the liner fit the excavation's contours. Then, I filled the trench with a mixture of half compost and half excavated soil, packing it down as I went, until it mounded in the center. It is important to fill the entire trench level by level to insure that the liner falls into place evenly along the entire length, and to tamp down the soil as you go.

Because small excavations dry out quickly, make your bog garden as large as possible. It should be at least 2½ feet deep.

OTHER WAYS TO BUILD A BOG

Bog gardens can be difficult to work into the landscape. If you have a pool or pond, place the bog garden next to it, so that the bog blends harmoniously into the landscape. If you connect the bog and the pool with a length of pipe to allow the water to flow freely, the pond can provide water for the bog. This will also keep water levels in both enclosures constant.

If you don't have room for an in-ground bog, you can still have a bog garden. Try using an old whiskey barrel or other container that holds water. I have seen kids' wading pools, utility sinks and even old bathtubs used to make bog gardens. Your imagination is the limit. With a little ingenuity, anyone can have an artificial bog garden. So what are you waiting for?

You can poke drainage holes around the liner, about a foot from the top, to keep plant crowns from rotting.

Some people install perforated pipes in the corners of the bog to expedite watering. The pipe is buried vertically, with the bottom of the pipe extending down to just above the bottom of the liner. The top of the pipe sits 1 to 2 inches above the soil line. There are two ways to do this: The simplest is to use narrow, perforated tubing and run a hose inside of it to water the bog. However, water can run into the bog too quickly, backing up in the tube. The second method requires two perforated pipes. Place a narrow tube within a larger tube at least 10 inches in diameter. Fill the gap between the two with pea gravel. When watering, run your garden hose down the inner tube. This methods enables the water to seep into the soil more gradually. It is particularly useful for controlling the water flow in specialized acidic bog gardens (see "A Bog for Specialized Plants," page 54).

I chose not to use pipes at all. My house has no gutters and so the bog, which runs the length of one side of the structure, collects all the water that runs off the roof each time it rains.

After adding the soil, I filled the new bog garden with tapwater and let it sit until the soil settled. I recommend waiting at least a month before planting, keeping the soil wet at all times. If you cannot wait a month — and few of us have such patience — wait at least a week. Smooth out the lumps in the the soil surface, keeping the mound in the center before you plant. Fill in with additional soil if necessary to keep a consistent level. Cut the plastic liner flush with the soil and you will never notice the seam between bog and lawn.

BOG PLANTS

Many of the plants that grow in the wet, peaty soils of bogs and other wetlands are beautiful garden plants for either sun or shade. Locate your bog according to which plants you wish to grow and how they fit in with the rest of your garden.

The bog garden includes astilbes, 'Hyperion' daylily, ligularia and Virginia sweet-spire. Topdressing with compost keeps the soil moist and rich.

In nature, a bog contains plants that are uniquely adapted to wet, acidic soils — acidic because little or no water flows through the bog and so no acids are leached away. In an artificial bog, you can either grow these specialized plants or a wide variety of perennials, bulbs and shrubs which require constantly moist soils, such as bog rosemary, turtlehead and blue flag iris. I chose the latter approach for my garden. Building a specialized bog garden is discussed on the next page. Before buying plants, decide on which kinds you wish to grow, either garden plants or those suited to acid conditions.

The beauty of bog plants is not just in their flowers, but also in their foliage. I love their bold showy leaves — the arrowhead shapes, the umbrellas and the swords — which is why I love bog gardens. These shapes are even more striking when contrasted with delicate sedges and ferns, which also thrive in moist soil.

MAINTENANCE

The most important maintenance job for an artificial bog garden is watering. Never let the soil dry out. Dry soil means sure death for moisture-loving plants. Mulch the garden with pine straw or oak leaves in the winter to help protect delicate plants. Leave the mulch in place, allowing it to rot into the soil. Top dressing with rich compost will also enrich the soil, keeping its level constant as the soil settles. As with any garden, remove weed seedlings before they become a problem. Weeds will be few as many of them do not thrive in wet soil. Depending on the location of your garden, tree seedlings may be a nuisance.

A BOG FOR SPECIALIZED PLANTS

Growing plants native to sterile acid bogs requires a different approach from the one I took in my garden. The environment of a true bog is unlike a low, wet woodland or meadow. A bog forms slowly in a glacial lake bed with the help of specialized mosses called sphagnum that grow inward from the edges of the lake. As they grow, the lower portions of their stems die but remain attached as the upper stems branch and spread, creating an interwoven mat.

At first the moss floats on the surface of the water. But as the mat grows and decays, it deposits peat on the lake bottom. As the sphagnum spreads outward, the floating mat becomes thick enough for other plants to take root and grow. Eventually, the sphagnum covers the entire lake, and the floating mat of vegetation is dense enough to support flowers, shrubs and even trees.

This kind of bog is called a quaking bog. Walking on it is like walking on a squishy waterbed. The ground trembles or quakes. To re-create this environment in your yard, you need to provide a sterile substrate on which the plants can grow. Clean, medium-coarse sand and peat moss are the best choices. Dig a trench as described in the accompanying chapter. Since most specialized bog plants

Pitcher plants such as yellow *Sarracenia flava*, above, and purple-veined *S. leucophylla*, opposite page, are becoming rare in the wild, so purchase them only from reputable dealers who propagate the plants they sell.

have sparse root systems, two feet is generally deep enough. I recommend installing perforated pipe in at least two corners of the bog as you may be adding distilled water or rainwater collected elsewhere. A pipe 2 to 4 inches in diameter is ideal. For larger bogs, use the double-pipe system described on page 52.

Fill the excavation with a 50/50 mixture of sphagnum and sand. A living layer of sphagnum at the top of the bog is desirable but may be hard to come by. Carolina Biological Supply Company is a good source. You can reach them at 2700 York Road, Burlington, N.C. 27215; (800) 334-5551.

It is imperative that you let the bog settle for at least a month before planting. The pH of the sand and sphagnum mix and the water need to come into balance before the plants are added. The additional time also allows the soil to settle. If it settles too much after the plants are established, it may bend or break their new roots.

Before planting, wash all the soil from the roots of the new plants to avoid introducing soil-borne microorganisms and worms. If you use live moss, add it after the other plants are in place. The moss is often slow to establish.

Use only rainwater or distilled

water in the bog. Tapwater contains minerals and chlorine harmful to bog plants. It is also neutral to alkaline in pH, and bog plants need a highly acidic soil. As with all bogs, consistent water is essential. Bogs are naturally low in nutrients, so do not add fertilizer.

Because it requires so much diligent attention, a specialized bog is not for everyone. Do not waste time and doom plants to a slow death if you are unwilling to manage a true bog garden properly.

Many bog plants, such as pitcher plants, are becoming rare in the wild. If you choose to plant them, purchase them only from reputable dealers who propagate their own plants. Make sure you do not buy wild-collected specimens. Remember that "nursery-grown" does not mean nursery *propagated*.

A living mulch of sphagnum moss is desirable for an acid bog. Add an additional mulch of pine straw in winter to protect delicate plants, especially in areas where winters are cold and snowfall is erratic. Remove the mulch in the spring to allow the sphagnum to grow.

PLANTS FOR THE ACID BOG

HERBACEOUS PLANTS

Calla palustris, Wild calla
Carex muskingumensis, Palm sedge
Clintonia borealis, Beadlily
Dionaea muscipula, Venus' flytrap
Drosera spp., Sundew
Eriophorum spp., Cottongrass
Gaultheria hispidula, Snowberry
Linnaea borealis, Twinflower
Osmunda spp., Cinnamon and royal
    ferns and other species
Sabatia spp., Marsh pink
Sarracenia spp., Pitcher plant
Thelypteris palustris, Marsh fern
Tofieldia spp., Bog asphodel

WOODY PLANTS

Andromeda polifolia var. *glaucophylla*, Bog rosemary
Chamaedaphne calyculata,
    Leatherleaf
Ilex verticillata, Winterberry holly
Kalmia angustifolia and *K. polifolia,*
    Bog laurel
Larix laricina, Larch
Ledum groenlandicum,
    Labrador tea
Myrica gale, Sweet gale
Picea mariana, Black spruce
Rhododendron canadense, Rhodora
Vaccinium macrocarpon, Cranberry

Stabilizing & Restoring Streambanks – Naturally

BY THOMAS S. BENJAMIN

PROPERTY OWNERS OFTEN REACT in alarm to erosion, shoring up disappearing streambanks exclusively with "hard," non-living materials like rock and environmentally damaging concrete and rubber tires. But the erosion of soil by running water is a natural and indeed inevitable process. Bioengineering is a natural, environment-friendly and aesthetically pleasing approach to controlling stream erosion. It minimizes the use of hard materials, using primarily plants and organic materials to stabilize banks, improve water quality and restore and enhance wildlife habitats. The intensive planting techniques used in bioengineering provide all the benefits of vegetative cover much more quickly than conventional planting techniques do.

The term bioengineering describes several methods of establishing plant cover by embedding a combination of live, dormant and/or decaying plant materials into the banks of streams and rivers. Inherently flexible and versatile, it can be adapted easily to specific situations. The methods and materials outlined in this chapter may be used separately or in various combinations to fit the great diversity of erosion conditions — from minor erosion along the streambanks on small lots to miles of eroding embankment along the bluffs of large lakes, reservoirs and rivers.

Bioengineering uses vegetation and organic materials such as coconut-fiber mats embedded with plants to stabilize banks, improve water quality and enhance wildlife habitat.

IS THERE AN EROSION PROBLEM?

Erosion can pose enormous difficulties to homeowners with developed land close to river or streambanks. Often development unnaturally causes or exacerbates erosion. Rather than seep into the soil as it does in vegetated areas, water on impervious paved surfaces concentrates in existing natural channels and constructed channels, conduits or pipes, gathering speed and force. When released into a river or stream, this increased volume can cause considerable unnatural erosion.

To determine if the erosion of your river or streambank is indeed a problem, start by considering which way the channel "wants" to flow and at what rate. Before calling in professionals, get a sense of what's happening on your own. Monitor your site for changes and keep track of where and how quickly they are occurring.

Determining whether or not you have an erosion problem is a personal decision based on how much you value the land versus the body of water that is causing it to erode. However, you should bring in professionals to analyze the forces at work on a site, determine why erosion is occurring and assess what can be done about it.

THE CAUSES OF EROSION

The causes of erosion vary widely. Flooding, either one time or chronic, is a primary cause. During either a major storm or flash flood banks may be "overtopped," causing soil runoff to increase. Land development and unnaturally powerful discharges from stormwater sewers increase the likelihood of flash floods and therefore may also result in erosion.

Coconut-fiber tubes called "biologs" shore up an eroding streambank.

The physical alteration of a stream's natural flow patterns due to flow-control structures or obstructions such as roads, dams, tide gates or weirs may lead to problems, even causing the stream's flow to reverse. Development — on-site or upstream — typically results in the unnaturally rapid build-up of silt and sediment which can clog waterways and cause erosion along adjacent banks. Wave impact caused by boating, wind, tidal flow and backflow in dammed and channeled areas is another cause of erosion. Finally, the denuding of banks either by trampling or clearing, overgrazing, fire, disease, storms or rock and landslides may lead to erosion.

A natural state is a dynamic state, constantly changing and evolving. Because erosion occurs naturally and is often inevitable, bioengineering isn't guaranteed to permanently stop the process, only to slow it down and minimize its impact.

Typical erosion conditions include:

• Undercutting at a bank bottom — scouring at the bottom of the bank, creating a hollowed-out trough under the bank itself. The upper bank becomes unstable and prone to collapse onto the scoured area.

- Shearing along a bank — removal of the bank in a lateral fashion, parallel to the direction of flow.
- Sloughing along a bank — large chunks of bank breaking off into the water. Characteristic of soft, alluvial soils. Often the result of scouring at the toe or bottom of the bank, which is where erosion often takes place.
- Upper-slope erosion — excessive soil loss, generally in specific spots along the upper portions of banks. This may also occur as a uniform condition across the entire length of the bank.

WHAT'S RIGHT AT THE SITE?

The first step in determining the degree and cause of erosion along your stream bank is to examine the site's existing environmental conditions. Fixing what is *not* working on your eroding streambank requires a thorough examination of what *is* working. This is especially true for the site's vegetation, as bioengineering treatments are strongly guided by existing plant cover. Bioengineered plantings can complement and enhance the existing environment by increasing the diversity of both plant and animal life and the area's aesthetic appeal. The following are many of the existing environmental conditions that professionals consider when evaluating a site:

GEOMORPHOLOGY
River or stream geomorphology is the result of geology, vegetation and the hydrologic forces that shape a channel and dictate how it will move and change over time. These factors need to be considered to determine where erosion is occurring (for example, on an outer bend, below a waterfall, in a narrow channel section) and why.

HYDROLOGY
Understanding the hydrological patterns of a river or stream is essential when bioengineering alternatives are being considered. The frequency and volume of high and low flows, typical and extreme inundation periods and water levels, as well as typical and extreme flow velocities are all key determinants. Whether or not plantings will be appropriate, which species should be used, where on the bank they should be placed and in what form they should come are determined largely by the site's hydrology.

A coconut-fiber tube laid horizontally along an eroding streambank acts as a secure planting medium for wetland seedlings. New installations need to be watered and protected from burrowing or overgrazing wildlife.

WATER QUALITY

The stream's water quality will also be a factor in choosing the type of treatment and selecting plants. Many wetland species are sensitive to water pollution and can tolerate only low levels of toxins (such as synthetic or inorganic chemicals) or nutrients (such as nitrogen and phosphorus). Other species not only tolerate but actually benefit from nutrient-rich waters (for example, cattails) — often to the detriment of more sensitive plants. Excessive silt and sediment also constitute pollution in streams and will affect the course of action.

SOILS

The preservation of your streambank's soils is the primary goal of bioengineering. Therefore, identifying the soil types and characteristics is imperative. Does your bank consist of sand, gravel or clay soil, or a combination? Is it natural or

These pre-vegetated fiber mats, planted with herbaceous seedlings, establish instant cover and quickly stabilize an eroded bank.

man-made fill? Is the soil at the bottom of the bank different from that at the top? The physical and chemical properties of the soils will directly influence plant selection.

EXISTING VEGETATION

Consider the overall nature and density of the vegetative cover. Is the site forested, scrubby, grassy, denuded or a mixture of these? How are different levels of the bank vegetated; is there a difference from top to bottom? Are plants well rooted, particularly at the bottom of the bank? What plant species are most common? Does the site appear to be in transition from one dominant species or plant type to another? How diverse is the vegetation? Do large trees appear to be leaning in any particular direction and are they becoming uprooted? Are any rare or endangered species present? Consider which plants are most appropriate: Grasses and herbaceous wildflowers are most suitable on small banks with low gradients, whereas woody species are best on steeper, larger banks.

These cardinal flowers are growing out of a coconut-fiber log. Within several weeks, the plants roots grow through the log and into the soil.

MICROCLIMATE

Particularly important for vegetation selection is the site's exposure to sun and prevailing winds. A sunny, calm site offers the greatest range of treatment and planting possibilities, while the opposite is true for shadier, windier sites. Consider the feasibility of improving solar access on shady sites.

TREATMENT TYPES AND MATERIALS

Once the erosion conditions, their causes and the environmental context of your site are thoroughly examined, the process of designing and installing an appropriate treatment can begin. The great range of materials used in bioengineering make the method adaptable to a wide variety of erosion conditions. Some commonly used materials include a combination of herbaceous and woody wetland species, such as grasses, sod, seed, brush, shrubs and coir, a coconut fiber.

No two bioengineering treatments are exactly the same because no two sites are the same. However, some common treatment combinations for light to severe erosion conditions are shown on the opposite page. For example, a slight slope with light to moderate erosion and minor water-level fluctuations may be treated with "pre-vegetated mattress" (coir or coconut fiber wrapped with mesh or fiber webbing and planted with herbaceous plants or special wetland sod). This establishes instant cover and quickly stabilizes the bank. For a steeper slope eroded by moderate to heavy wave action, coir fascine, a cylindrical structure (typically about 20 feet long and a foot in diameter) consisting of coir and wrapped with either coir or synthetic mesh, may be used in addition to rock to stabilize the bank and create a breakwater at its base or toe. A combination of coir mesh and brush (stems cut from living wetland shrubs) may be planted above the fascine.

On a level to moderate slope with severe erosion and poor soils, rock and brush mattressing (mattress-like structures made of intertwined dead branches) may be the best choice. If available, large, dead tree trunks (coarse woody debris) may be added to help stabilize the lower bank.

The various treatments can be secured to the bank in different ways, depending on the situation. Securing methods range from wood stakes and twine to rebar drilled through the material and into the substrate. Abrupt transitions between different materials and different sections of the same materials should be avoided, both for the sake of durability and aesthetics.

Many of the upland species used to revegetate the top of a bank are readily available at nurseries. However, herbaceous wetland plants can be obtained only through a limited number of specialized suppliers (see "Nursery Sources," page 104). Most live brush used for bioengineering purposes is not grown in containers but harvested from trees and shrubs growing in the wild and can be purchased from specialized suppliers. The bottom two-thirds of the cuttings are submerged in the soil, where they take root. Dead brush is sometimes used as a temporary breakwater to slow the flow of water on a steep slope until the other planted materials can take hold.

MAINTENANCE

Maintenance is as important for a newly installed bioengineered treatment where living material has been used as it is for a newly planted lawn or garden. The plants need regular watering, particularly during hot or dry spells. New treatments also need protection from burrowing wildlife and from overgrazing by waterfowl, particularly geese. This protection can take a variety of forms. For example, simple wood

EROSION SEVERITY AND SOLUTIONS

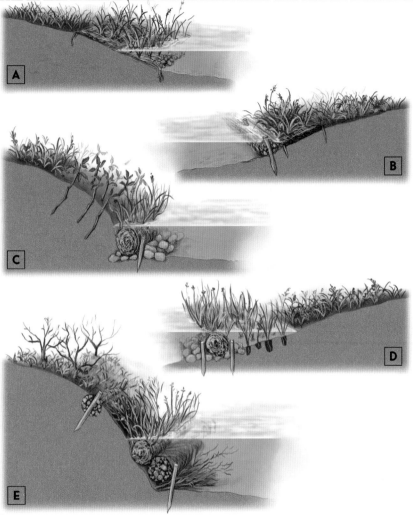

A A slight slope with minor erosion and water-level fluctuations may be treated with "pre-vegetated mattresses" directly behind the breakwater. **B** A slightly steeper slope eroded by moderate to heavy waves is treated with brush fascine at the base with live staking above. **C** For a moderate slope with severe erosion and poor soils, rock and wood staking is used at the base with a coir mattress above and live staking on the upper bank. **D** Extreme erosion along streams subject to flash flooding are treated with rock, wood staking and coir fascine at the base and fiber mats on the upper bank. **E** On a steep slope with severe erosion, mattress-like structures made of dead branches are installed at the base, followed by rock and brush fascine, with brush mattresses above the waterline.

Bioengineering treatments can be secured to the bank using different materials. Stems cut from live shrubs are used on the middle to upper bank.

Branches are also used in fascines, or tightly rolled bundles. These are staked into narrow terraces to shore up the middle or upper bank.

staking tied with string can deter waterfowl. Wildlife netting draped over newly installed vegetation will keep away birds and deer. Piles of fine woody debris and small brush on top of newly vegetated areas will discourage geese from landing.

New installations need to be protected, too, from trampling by humans and pets. Snow fencing is one effective deterrent. Thorny shrubs like raspberries and roses (which have the added feature of supplying food and cover for wildlife, birds and insects) make good barrier plantings, as do some grasses, including rice cut grass (*Leersia oryzoides*).

At this location, a combination of materials was used: a brush mattress of willows and dogwoods was laid on biodegradable blankets behind coconut-fiber logs.

WETLAND PLANTS

The plant encyclopedia that follows is divided into regions, each with its own distinctive wetland flora. Fifteen particularly spectacular plants are highlighted for each region, with information on salient characteristics as well as growing and design tips. These highlighted plants are followed by comprehensive regional lists of native plants that offer a diverse palette for a delightful natural water garden.

Both the USDA and Sunset zones are provided for each featured plant. For a USDA hardiness zone map, consult any reliable garden encyclopedia or other reference. If you live in the West, consult the detailed maps in *Sunset Western Garden Book*, published by the editors of Sunset Books and Sunset magazine.

WETLAND PLANTS

For the Northeast & Middle Atlantic

BY JUDY GLATTSTEIN

NATURAL WETLANDS in this region — wooded streamsides, moist forest areas, some marshes and bogs — have been reduced by past agricultural practices such as ditching and draining. They continue to fall victim to highway construction and the proliferation of shopping malls. Often the predominant tree of local wetlands is red maple. Shade-tolerant shrubs include two that have made the rare transition from wildling to popular cultivated shrub — summersweet and winterberry holly. Ferns, marsh marigold and skunk cabbage are but a few of the woodland wetland denizens growing on the forest floor. Sunny wetlands have their own characteristic flora, including swamp milkweed, a pink-flowered relative of the upland species and equally attractive to butterflies.

Sweet flag, *Acorus calamus*
Bright green leaves look much like those of a cattail. Flowers are small and inconspicuous, in a small spike on the side of a leaf-like stalk. Native from Canada south to Florida, and coast to coast. The foliage of sweet flag contrasts nicely with that of ferns in sunny, shallow-water situations. A variegated form, *A. c. variegatas*, is also available. Zones: USDA 2-10, Sunset all zones.

Summersweet, *Clethra alnifolia*

A shade- and moisture-tolerant shrub valuable for its late blooming period. Spikes of white or pink, deliciously fragrant flowers appear in mid to late summer. Stoloniferous growth results in thickets of 8' to 10' tall stems. Persistent seed capsules lend winter interest. Readily available at nurseries. Zones: USDA 4-10, Sunset 2-6.

Witchhazel

Summersweet

Witchhazel, *Hamamelis virginiana*

An autumn-flowering species with narrow ribbon-like petals and spicy-scented flowers. Shrubs have an open vase-like shape, reaching 12' tall at maturity. Useful for informal plantings at woodland edges. Attractive foliage turns clear yellow in fall. Deer do not seem to browse on witchhazel. Zones: USDA 4-8, Sunset 1-9, 14-16, 18-21.

Dwarf fothergilla, *Fothergilla gardenii*

Prefers light shade and requires a moist site. White flowers resembling small bottlebrushes appear in spring at the same time as the leaves. Shrubs grow 4' tall in shade, even more compactly with some sun, which also causes more intense autumn leaf color of orange, red and gold. Zones: USDA 4-9, Sunset 3-9, 14-17.

Winterberry holly, *Ilex verticillata*

Of great winter interest, when the dark twiggy branches are covered with vivid red berries that persist until spring. Plants are dioecious: female plants bear the berries but a nearby male plant is necessary for pollination. Use winterberry along pond edges or other damp sites. Named forms are available. Zones: USDA 3-8, Sunset 3-9, 11-24.

Cardinal Flower

Blue Flag Iris

Blue flag iris, *Iris versicolor*
Handsome and easy to grow, with narrow, sword-like, glaucous blue-green leaves about 2' tall. Slate-blue flowers in May and early June. Suitable for sunny wet meadows, ditches, swales or moist soil bordering a pond. Plant in groups for best effect. Zones: USDA 2-8, Sunset 1-9, 14-24.

Spicebush, *Lindera benzoin*
Numerous clusters of small, chartreuse flowers decorate bare branches in early spring. Aromatic, spicy-scented leaves turn clear yellow in autumn. Female plants have attractive red berries similar to those of a flowering dogwood. Requires shade and moisture to thrive. May take some searching to find a nursery source. Zones: USDA 5-9, Sunset 3-9, 14-24.

Cardinal flower, *Lobelia cardinalis*
Showy perennial with vivid red flowers that bloom on 3' stems late summer. Provide a moist to wet site in partial shade to full sun. Plants are susceptible to winter kill so provide a light airy mulch of pine boughs or oak leaves held in place with chicken wire. Zones: USDA 3-9, Sunset 1-7, 12-17.

Ostrich fern, *Matteucia struthiopteris*
Clusters of stately fronds up to 5' tall grow in rich, moist soil. Underground runners spread to make sizeable colonies. Brown and woody fertile fronds, usually 2' tall, appear in late June or early July and persist through the winter months, lending seasonal interest. Zones: USDA 3-8, Sunset 1-10, 14-24.

Sensitive fern, *Onoclea sensibilis*
A freely running deciduous fern suitable as a ground cover for moist sites. Bold, tropical-looking fronds 15" tall or

more are produced through spring and summer, turning yellow with frost. Sterile fronds, like beaded sticks, persist through winter and provide a second season of interest. Zones: USDA 3-10, Sunset 1-9, 14-24.

Cinnamon Fern

Virginia chain fern,
Woodwardia virginica
Begins its growth later in spring than other ferns. The deciduous fertile and sterile fronds are similar, 18" to 24" tall with dark green pinnae. Rhizomes quickly spread to form large mats in the marshy, swampy sites that the plant favors. With ample moisture, this fern can grow in full sun. Zones: USDA 4-10, Sunset 4-9, 14-24.

Pickerel Rush

Cinnamon fern, *Osmunda cinnamomea*
A stately, 4' tall, clump-forming fern for shaded, wet sites. In autumn, sterile fronds turn a rich straw-gold. Fertile fronds look like dense masses of cinnamon-brown spores and fade away after the spores are shed. Elegant as an accent plant or in masses. Zones: USDA 2-11, Sunset 1-9, 14-24.

Pickerel rush, *Pontederia cordata*
Dense spikes of beautiful blue-violet flowers bloom in July and August. Plant in sunny, shallow water along pond edges and slow-moving streams. Plants grow 2' feet tall, and quickly form dense colonies from branching rhizomes. Leaves are arrow-shaped, similar to arrow arum. Zones: USDA 3-10, Sunset all zones.

71

Swamp azalea, *Rhododendron viscosum*

Valuable for its late blooming season, with intensely fragrant white or pinkish flowers in early to mid-summer. This shrub has sparse, deciduous foliage. Leaves turn a soft orange before falling. Tolerant of wet, shady conditions, swamp azalea is becoming more widely available at nurseries. Zones: USDA 3-9, Sunset 3-9, 14-24.

Arrow Arum

Arrow arum, *Peltandra virginica*

Happiest in shady, wet sites such as swamps and the banks of slow-moving streams. Grow this 3' tall plant for its handsome, arrow-shaped leaves up to 18" long. Provides an elegant contrast to ferns. The flowers look like small greenish white calla lilies. Zones: USDA 4-9, Sunset 3-9, 14-24.

MORE WETLAND PLANTS FOR

THE NORTHEAST & MIDDLE ATLANTIC

TREES

Asimina triloba, Pawpaw
Amelanchier laevis, Shadbush
Betula nigra, River birch
Fraxinus nigra, Black ash
Larix laricina, Tamarack or Eastern larch
Liquidambar styraciflua, Sweet gum
Nyssa sylvatica, Black or sour gum, tupelo
Picea mariana, Black spruce
Quercus palustris, Pin oak
Thuja occidentalis, Eastern white cedar or Eastern arborvitae

SHRUBS

Cephalanthus occidentalis, Buttonbush
Cornus amomum, Silky dogwood
Cornus stolonifera, Red-osier dogwood
Dirca palustris, Leatherwood
Ledum groenlandicum, Labrador tea
Rhododendron arborescens, Sweet azalea
Rhododendron maximum, Rosebay rhododendron
Rosa palustris, Swamp rose
Salix discolor, Pussy willow
Sambucus canadensis, American elderberry
Viburnum dentatum, Arrowwood
Viburnum trilobum, American cranberry bush

PERENNIALS

Arisaema dracontium, Green dragon
Arisaema triphyllum, Jack-in-the-pulpit
Asclepias incarnata , Swamp milkweed
Calla palustris, Wild calla
Caltha palustris, Marsh marigold
Camassia cusickii, Camassia
Chelone glabra, White turtlehead
Coptis trifolia ssp. *groenlandica*,
    Goldthread
Dodecatheon meadia, Shooting-star
Eupatorium maculatum, Joe-pye weed
Helianthus angustifolius, Swamp
    sunflower
Hibiscus palustris, Marsh mallow
Hypericum virginicum, Marsh
    St.-John's-wort
Lilium canadense, Canada lily
Lilium superbum, Turk's cap lily
Lobelia syphilitica, Blue lobelia
Lysimachia terrestris, Swamp candles
Menyanthes trifoliata, Bog bean
Mertensia virginica, Virginia bluebells
Mimulus guttatus, Monkey musk
Monarda didyma, Oswego tea
Nymphaea odorata, White water-lily
Orontium aquaticum, Golden-club
Pontederia cordata, Pickerel rush
Potentilla palustris, Marsh cinquefoil
Rudbeckia laciniata, Cut-leaf coneflower
Sagittaria latifolia, Duck potato
Saururus cernuus, Lizard's-tail
Senecio aureus, Golden ragwort
Silphium laciniatum, Cup plant
Sisyrinchium angustifolium, Blue-eyed
    grass

Solidago uliginosa, Marsh goldenrod
Thalictrum pubescens Tall meadow rue
Tradescantia virginiana, Spiderwort
Vernonia noveboracensis, Common
    ironweed
Veronicastrum virginicum, Culver's root
Xyris iridifolia, Yellow-eyed grass
Zizia aurea, Golden alexander

GRASSES & GRASS-LIKE PLANTS

Carex muskingumensis, Palm sedge
Carex paniculata, Panicled sedge
Carex pendula, Drooping sedge
Carex stipata, Tussock sedge
Eriophorum angustifolium, Narrow-
    leaved cotton grass
Eriophorum latifolium, Broad-leaved
    cotton grass
Poa palustris, Fowl meadow grass
Scirpus tabernaemontani, Bulrush

FERNS

Athyrium filix-femina, Lady fern
Athyrium pycnocarpon, Glade fern
Dryopteris goldiana, Goldie's wood fern
Osmunda claytonia, Interrupted fern
Osmunda regalis, Royal fern
Phegopteris connectilis, Northern beech
    fern
Thelypteris palustris, Marsh fern

73

WETLAND PLANTS

For the Southeast & Deep South

BY LOGAN CALHOUN

THE WETLANDS OF THIS vast region stretching from the plains of Texas and Oklahoma to the southeastern seaboard and down to the Gulf of Mexico are diverse, encompassing flatwoods, bottomlands, streamsides, bogs and swamps. Indigenous plants are the best choices because they're adapted to the region's climatic extremes. Winters are warm with occasional "Blue Northerns," arctic high-pressure systems that can cause temperatures to plummet 60 degrees or more. Six months a year, days and nights are unrelentingly hot and humid. Generally, soils are highly alkaline in the west and highly acidic in the south and southeast, with the exception of delta areas of the Gulf coast, where they are neutral to alkaline. Periodically, these soils become saturated with rain water, and at other times drought causes them to crack.

Southern swamp maple,
Acer rubrum var. *drummondii*
A harbinger of spring. Red blooms burst open on bare branches in February or March, followed by attractive red samaras dangling in clusters. Foliage produces cooling summer shade and in autumn turns a stunning combination of red and gold. Best grown with roots in constantly moist soil. Found in low woods, bottomlands and wooded swamps from southeast

Oklahoma to Florida. Zones: USDA 5-10, Sunset 1-9, 14-17.

Southern Maidenhair Fern

Southern maidenhair fern,
Adiantum capillus-veneris

Produces delicate lime-green fronds with jet black stipes. Evergreen nature makes this fern valuable as a year-round foil around rocks and water sources. A lacy little plant that graces seep springs, floodplains, clay-filled bottomlands and outcroppings throughout the South, from the Edward's Plateau to Florida, north to North Carolina. Zones: USDA 6-11, Sunset 5-9, 14-24.

Crossvine, *Bignonia capreolata*

A large evergreen vine covered with gorgeous, 2" trumpet-shaped flowers in shades of yellow and red. Blooms sporadically from spring to late fall, most abundantly in full sun. Glossy, deep green leaves. Found in bottomlands from Missouri to the Gulf coast,

and east to Florida. Zones: USDA 6-11, Sunset 5-9, 14-24.

Swamp lily, *Crinum americanum*

Coarse, glossy, strap-like foliage up to 3' long. Pink buds open to 5" white, star-shaped flowers from late summer until November. Flowers are held close to the ground on 3" to 4" stalks. This lovely lily is native to coastal swamps from Texas to western Florida and prefers to be submerged. Zones: USDA 7-11, Sunset 8,9, 12-24.

Stokes Aster

Stokes aster, *Stokesia laevis*

Produces an abundance of 2" to 3" ragged-petaled flowers over a prolonged period from June to September. Flowers in shades of indigo, azure or white are carried in open clusters on 8" to 12" stems. Leaves are lance-shaped, medium green, with a central white stripe and form a tight rosette. Requires partial shade to full sun and moist soil. Found in roadside

75

ditches and wet meadows from east Texas to Florida and Georgia. Zones: USDA 6-9, Sunset 1-9, 12-24.

Possumhaw

Possumhaw, *Ilex decidua*

Medium to large shrub native throughout the South in flood plains and on streambanks. Yellow to red berries are stunning on bare branches during the winter season. Berries are an excellent source of food for birds and other wildlife. Creamy white flowers are insignificant. Only female shrubs produce berries. Zones: USDA 5-11, Sunset 2-9, 15, 16, 19-23.

Sugarcane plume grass,
Saccharum (Erianthus) giganteum

Large grass averages 5' to 6' tall and rivals the common pampas grass in ornamental qualities. Silvery pink plumes last from late summer to mid-autumn. Basal foliage forms a dense, medium green tussock. Requires full sun and constantly moist or submerged roots. Found on shady roadsides, savannas, marshes and low woods from Texas to Florida, north to North Carolina. Zones: USDA 7-11, Sunset 8, 9, 12-24.

Texas copper lily,
Habranthus tubispathus

A small golden rainlily in the amaryllis family that blooms from mid-summer until November with every rain. The 2-1/2" copper-yellow flowers are carried on 10" stems above shiny green, reed-like foliage. Give this jewel full sun and moist soil. Texas copper lily is native from northeast Texas to the Coastal Bend in savannas and low woods. Zones: USDA 7-11, Sunset 8, 9, 12-24.

Louisiana iris, *Iris* x *louisiana*

Arguably the most beautiful and versatile wetland plant of the South. Originated from crosses between the copper iris (*Iris fulva*) and several other southern species. Colors and patterns of blooms are exquisite in the spring, while evergreen foliage adds a vertical accent the rest of the year. Plants should be placed in moist soil and full sun for the best show. Zones: USDA 5-11, Sunset 3-24.

Seashore mallow,
Kosteletzkya virginica

A 4' to 10' tall perennial with a hibiscus-like flower. Normally pink, the flowers may also be lavender or white. When grown in full sun and constantly moist soil, the plant flowers profusely. May bloom from June until October. Plant in masses. Native to coastal marshes, both fresh and brackish, from southern Delaware to eastern Texas. Zones: USDA 6-11, Sunset 8, 9, 12-24.

Southern wax myrtle,
Myrica cerifera
Among the finest evergreen shrubs in the South. Olive green and highly aromatic foliage with bayberry-like scent. In summer, female plants produce blue-gray berries prized by many birds. Can be used as a screen or a landscape specimen. Prefers moist soil, but tolerates inundation. Found in coastal wetlands, dunes and low woods from Arkansas and the Florida keys, north to southern Maryland. Zones: USDA 6-11, Sunset 5-9, 14-24.

Floating heart,
Nymphoides aquatica
Perfect floater for a small garden where a water-lily might be too aggressive. Half-inch white flowers appear from May to September. Plants cover an average of 6" square of the water's surface. Should be placed in full sun or part shade. Found in still, open water from coastal Texas to Florida, north to North Carolina. Zones: USDA 6-11, Sunset 7-9, 12-24.

Mexican water-lily,
Nymphaea mexicana
Yellow-flowered lily spectacular both in its own right and as a parent of many new hybrids. Less aggressive than *Nyphaea odorata*, so it will not take over small ponds. Place in full sun. Native to still, open water in Texas and Mexico. Zones: USDA 8-11, Sunset 9, 12-24.

Dwarf palmetto, *Sabal minor*
Lovely evergreen palm that adds a tropical accent in an aquatic landscape. Soil should be moist to boggy for best growth. Remarkably hardy, forming dense mounds of stiff fronds from stout subterranean trunks. Ultimate size varies with seed sources, normally from 4' to 10' high with an equal spread. Found in pine savannas and bottomlands from southeast Virginia to Florida, west to Oklahoma and Texas. Zones: USDA 6-11, Sunset 9-17, 19-24.

Floating Heart

Bald cypress, *Taxodium distichum*
The bell of Southern trees, will reach 40' to 60'. Ideally suited to wet areas. A light, airy, deciduous conifer that is equally at home on the water's edge or slightly submerged. Produces knees, knobby extensions that rise from the root for gas exchange if roots are submerged. The foliage turns bronzy yellow in autumn. Found in slow streams, pond margins, wooded swamps and bottomlands from the Edward's Plateau and Coastal Texas, east to Florida and Maryland. Zones: USDA 5-11, Sunset 2-10, 12-24.

Bald Cypress

MORE WETLAND PLANTS FOR

THE SOUTHEAST & DEEP SOUTH

TREES

Betula nigra, River birch
Gordonia lasianthus, Loblolly bay
Liquidambar styraciflua, Sweet gum
Magnolia virginiana, Sweetbay
Magnolia virginiana var. *australis,*
    Evergreen Sweetbay
Pinus taeda, Loblolly pine
Quercus nigra, Water oak
Quercus phellos, Willow oak
Sabal mexicana, Texas palm
Sabal palmetto, Cabbage palm

SHRUBS AND VINES

Avicennia germinans, Black mangrove
Baccharis angustifolia, False willow
Cephalanthus occidentalis, Buttonbush
Cyrilla racemiflora, Titi
Gelsemium sempervirens, Carolina
    jessamine
Ilex cassine, Dahoon holly
Ilex verticillata, Winterberry holly
Itea virginica, Sweetspire
Leucothoe (Agarista) populifolia,
    Andromeda
Lonicera sempervirens, Coral
    honeysuckle
Rhododendron oblongifolium, Sweet azalea

Rhododendron austrinum, Florida azalea

Rosa palustris, Swamp rose

PERENNIALS

Canna flaccida, Swamp canna

Eupatorium coelestinum, Blue mist flower

Equisetum hyemale, Horsetail

Helianthus angustifolius, Swamp
  sunflower

Hibiscus coccineus, Texas star hibiscus

Hibiscus militaris, Marsh mallow

Hibiscus laevis, Swamp mallow

Hymenocallis liriosome, Spider lily

Iris brevicaulis, Zig-Zag iris

Iris fulva, Red Louisiana iris

Iris giganticaerulea, Giant Louisiana iris

Iris hexagona, Blue southern iris

Iris nelsonii, Nelson's iris

Iris virginica, Swamp iris

Lobelia cardinalis, Cardinal flower

Monarda fistulosa, Bergamot

Nelumbo lutea, Yellow lotus

Nymphaea elegans, Blue water-lily

Nymphaea odorata, White fragrant water-
  lily

Peltandra virginica, Arrow-leaf

Penstemon tenuis, Gulf coast penstemon

Phlox divaricata, Louisiana phlox

Phlox pilosa, Prairie phlox

Physostegia angustifolia, Spring-blooming
  obedient plant

Physostegia virginiana, Fall-blooming
  obedient plant

Rudbeckia maxima, Giant coneflower

Salvia lyrata, Lyre-leaf sage

Sagittaria latifolia, Delta duckpotato

Saururus cernuus, Lizardtail

Thalia dealbata, Powdery thalia

Typha angustifolia, Cattail

Viola missouriensis, Missouri violet

Viola walteri, Walter's violet

GRASSES AND FERNS

Andropogon glomeratus, Bushy bluestem
  grass

Chasmanthus latifolium, Inland sea oats

Rhynchospora colorata, White star sedge

Muhlenbergia capillaris, Gulf muhly
  grass

Muhlenbergia lindheimeri, Lindheimer's
  muhly grass

Onoclea sensibilis, Sensitive fern

Osmunda regalis var. *spectabilis*, Royal
  fern

Osmunda cinnamomea, Cinnamon fern

Panicum virgatum, Switch grass

Polystichum acrostichoides, Christmas
  fern

Thelypteris kunthii, River fern

WETLAND PLANTS
For South Florida

BY GEORGIA TASKER

AT THE TURN OF THE CENTURY, the Everglades comprised nearly all of South Florida. Today, more than half of that wetlands system has been lost. But the state still has a dazzling array of watery environments: swamps, bogs, strands, sloughs, wet prairies and marshes. Freshwater marshes range from those that are nearly always standing in water to shallow and seasonally wet prairies. Tree islands called hammocks dot the marshes, and the soil of some of them is quite wet. Some pine flatwoods interlaced among the marshes and cypress swamps stand in water for a month or so during the summer rainy season. In South Florida, it is best to plant at the end of the dry season, in late May.

Red maple,

Acer rubrum var. *trilobum*

One of the few trees to provide autumn color in South Florida, the red maple is a temperate tree at the southern end of its range here. Fast-growing and tall with a narrow crown, leaves that shed in the fall, red flowers in winter and winged fruit or samaras in late winter. Commonly found in cypress swamps, or in waist-deep water during the wet season. Plant in saturated soil or water to six inches. Zones: USDA 7-10, Sunset 1-9, 14-17.

Leather fern,

Acrostichum danaeifolium

The largest fern in the U.S. with fronds up to 12' long, the leather fern's leaflets are beefy but brittle. These are often found in hydric hammocks or cypress stands, at the bases of trees. The leather fern doesn't like to dry out. Fiddleheads are edible and said to taste like asparagus, with the consistency of okra. Difficult to transplant from the wild. Plant in saturated soils. Zones: USDA 10-11, Sunset 16-24.

Pond Apple

Pond apple, *Annona glabra*

Easily recognized when in fruit because the yellow-green fruit is heart-shaped and hangs on the limbs like a Christmas ornament; a wonderful wildlife food source. Flower buds in spring are triangular; flowers have six creamy white petals, and three outer petals marked basally by a crimson dot. Plant where water meets the shore. Pond apples tolerate standing water for half the year. Zones: USDA 10-11, Sunset 16-24.

Swamp fern, *Blechnum serrulatum*

Large fronds with robust pinnae;

coarser looking than Boston or sword fern. Large stands grow around the bases of royal palms in the Fakahatchee Strand near the Big Cypress National Preserve. It is still possible to collect this fern from the wild, though many other endangered ferns are protected, so be sure you have its identity correct. Plant in saturated soils. Zones: USDA 10, Sunset 16-24.

Sawgrass

Sawgrass, *Cladium jamaicense*

The most prevalent sedge in the Everglades, named for its toothed edges. Marjory Stoneman Douglas wrote in *The Everglades, River of Grass*: "The miracle of the light pours over the green and brown expanse of sawgrass and water....the grass and the water that is the meaning and the central fact of the Everglades of Florida." The infloresence is taller than the leaves; branches with spikelets of flowers are brown. Can grow in 1' to 3' of water that stands for 6 to 9 months. Zones: USDA 8-11, Sunset 16-24.

Spike-rush

Swamp Hibiscus

Spike-rush, *Eleocharis cellulosa*
Really a round-leaved sedge, spike-rush grows in full sun in standing water. Generally darker green than the nearby vegetation, such as sagittaria or swamp lilies, and handsome all year. Small fish will take shelter among these stems in shallow water. Plant in soil that is saturated to about 6" deep. Zones: USDA 8-11, Sunset 16-24.

Myrsine, *Myrsine floridana*
From a tropical plant family, myrsine is found in pinelands and hammocks. Leaves are wavy, bright green and arranged in a spiral on the twigs, while the black fruits develop along bare branches. Plant around the edge of a wetland or water garden. Zones: USDA 9-10, Sunset 16-24.

Swamp hibiscus, *Hibiscus grandiflorus*
Pink-flowered hibiscus are conspicuous in the summer heat of cypress swamps. There also is a rare white form. Grows in standing water several months of the year, drying out in the natural dry season of late spring. Plant in partial shade to open sun in saturated soils on the edge of the water. Zones: USDA 9-11, Sunset 16-24.

Spatterdock, *Nuphar lutea* ssp. *advena*
Yellow petals look as if they are just about to open but never do. Instead, they curl up and over the ovary, like a cup, hiding stamens inside. Like water-lilies, spatterdocks float their leaves on the surface of still water. Occasionally submerged leaves occur. Flowers

only in full sun. Plant rhizomes in 2' to 4' of water. Zones: USDA 9-11, Sunset 16-24.

White water-lily, *Nymphaea odorata*
Has a lovely almond fragrance. Sensitive to herbicides as well as copper used to control algae. Found in sloughs or deep-water drainage areas of the marsh. Plant to a depth of 1' to 3', depending on pond size; deeper in larger ponds. Zones: USDA 7-10, Sunset 12-24.

Arrowhead, *Sagittaria lancifolia*
and *S. latifolia*
S. lancifolia has narrow leaves, while *S. latifolia* has larger, arrow-shaped leaves that grow 2' tall or more. White flowers with bright yellow stamens in whorls of three grow on tall, separate stems. Arrowhead mixes easily with pickerel weed and cattails in standing, shallow water. Plant these species in soil that is saturated to about 6" or 8" of water. Zones: USDA *S. lancifolia*, 6-11; *S. latifolia*, 6-10, Sunset both species, 1-9, 14-24.

Pond cypress, *Taxodium ascendens*
Little else matches the lovely fresh greenness of new leaves on cypress trees in spring and early summer. Flaky gray bark is often colored with lichens. Branches are upright and ascending. Found in stillwater swamps, rather than flowing water. Seedlings grow best in saturated soil,

not standing water, but mature trees can thrive in water 6 to 9 months a year. Plant in water up to 6" deep in full sun. Zones: USDA 8-10, Sunset 1-9, 16-24.

Marsh Pink

Marsh pink, *Sabatia* spp.
Found from the wet prairie to the pinelands, over a variety of conditions from seasonally to briefly inundated. In May, these delicate, lovely flowers are a marked contrast to the dry prairie floor beneath them. There is a white form and a large species with 10 petals. Plant in saturated soil. Zones: USDA 9-11, Sunset 16-24.

Alligator Flag

Alligator flag, *Thalia geniculata*
With canna-like leaves, alligator flags signal the deeper water of the cypress swamp where alligators are likely to be found. By mid-summer, these tall herbs are eaten and ragged. The inflorescence, which branches, may be twice the height of the leaves. Plant in 2' to 4' of water that stays flooded 6 to 9 months of the year. Zones: USDA 9-10, Sunset 16-24.

Cocoplum, *Chrysobalanus icaco*
Often found rimming alligator holes in the sawgrass marsh, cocoplum is a shrub or small tree. It has round to oval leaves which, on some forms, are red when new. Tiny white flowers occur year-round; fruit is a purple drupe and wildlife love it. Cocoplum also grows in swamps and hammocks. Plant in saturated soils, but not standing water. Zones: USDA 10-11, Sunset 16-24.

MORE WETLAND PLANTS FOR

SOUTH FLORIDA

TREES

Ficus aurea, Strangler fig
Fraxinus caroliniana, Pop ash
Ilex cassine, Dahoon holly
Magnolia virginiana,
     Sweet-bay magnolia
Persea borbonia, Red bay
Pinus elliottii var. *elliottii,* Slash pine
Quercus laurifolia, Laurel oak

PALMS

Acoelorraphe wrightii, Paurotis palm
Sabal palmetto, Cabbage or sabal palm
Serenoa repens, Saw palmetto

SHRUBS

Cephalanthus occidentalis, Buttonbush
Ilex glabra, Galberry
Myrica cerifera, Wax myrtle
Salix caroliniana, Coastal plains willow
Sambucus canadensis, Elderberry

FERNS

Osmunda regalis var. *spectabilis,* Royal
    fern
Thelypteris palustris, Marsh fern
Woodwardia virginica, Virginia chain fern

GRASSES AND WILDFLOWERS

Coelorachis rugosa, Wrinkled joint-tail
Coreopsis leavenworthii, Tickseed
Cyperus tetragonus, Cyperus
Eragrostis spp., Love grass
Saccharum (Erianthus) giganteum, Plume grass
Eustachys glauca, Marsh fingergrass
Eupatorium coelestinum, Blue mistflower
Helenium pinnatifidum, Everglades daisy
Juncus megacephalus, Juncus
Muhlenbergia capillaris, Muhly grass
Panicum hemitomon, Maidencane
Panicum hians, Gaping panicum
Rhynchospora colorata, White-topped sedge
Schoenus nigricans, Black rush
Scirpus tabernaemontani, Soft-stem bulrush
Setaria parviflora, Foxtail
Solidago stricta, Narrowleaf goldenrod
Spartina bakeri, Sand cordgrass
Tripsacum dactyloides, Fakahatchee grass

VINES

Ampelopsis arborea, Peppervine
Aster carolinianus, Climbing aster
Ipomoea sagittata, Everglades morning glory
Mikania scandens, Climbing hempweed
Parthenocissus quinquefolia, Virginia creeper
Smilax laurifolia, Catbriar
Vitis cinerea var. *floridana*, Pigeon grape

PERENNIALS

Aletris lutea, Yellow colic root
Canna flaccida, Golden canna
Crinum americanum, Swamp or string lily
Eriocaulon decangulare, Pipewort
Helenium pinnatifidum, Marsh sneezeweed
Hydrolea corymbosa, Skyflower
Hymenocallis palmeri, Alligator lily
Hypericum cistifolium, St. John's wort
Iva microcephala, Marsh elder
Lachnanthes caroliniana, Bloodroot
Lachnocaulon anceps, Bog-buttons
Lobelia glandulosa, Glades lobelia
Nymphoides aquatica, Floating hearts
Peltandra virginica, Green arum
Pontederia lanceolata, Pickerel weed
Potamogeton illinoensis, Pondweed
Pluchea rosea, Marsh fleabane
Rudbeckia hirta, Black-eyed Susan
Solidago stricta, Narrowleaf goldenrod
Teucrium canadense, Wood sage
Utricularia cornuta, Horned bladderwort
Utricularia foliosa, Bladderwort
Utricularia purpurea, Purple bladderwort

WETLAND PLANTS

For the Midwest & Great Plains

BY C. COLSTON BURRELL

DEEP PEATLANDS AND BOGS cover miles of country in the far northern reaches of this region. The northern plains are dominated by kettle wetlands formed in the wake of glaciers. The Canadian shield of the Great Lakes and boreal region are peppered with shallow, peaty wetlands over bedrock and laced with intricate threads of sluggish streams. The south has shallow wetlands, ponds, lakes and streams. Riparian systems cross the entire region. Gardeners here are primarily working with wildflowers, sedges, grasses and ferns, with some shrubs around wetland margins as they grade into the upland. Except in bogs and floodplains, there are few trees. The wetland gardens most appropriate for the Midwest are pools, ponds and bog gardens.

Canada bluejoint,

Calamagrostis canadensis

A finely textured grass with thin, blue-green blades on 1' to 3' stems. Soft, golden-brown plumes are carried above the leaves in early to mid-summer. They persist through the fall and into winter. Plants form extensive, dense colonies from creeping rhizomes. Found in low woods, marshes, wet prairies and bogs. Zones: USDA 2-7, Sunset 1-9, 14-22.

Wild Calla

Wild calla, *Calla palustris*
Borrows its name and good looks from its relative, the florist's calla. A small, snow white spathe surrounds the yellow spadix. Heart-shaped leaves are borne in an open rosette from a creeping rhizome. The stems and leaves are succulent and filled with airy tissue. Easy to grow in rich mucky soil that never dries out, or in standing water. Found in the shallow water of sluggish streams, bogs and wet ditches. Zones: USDA 2-6, Sunset 1-9, 14-20.

Joe-pye weed, *Eupatorium maculatum*
Colorful medicine man Joe-pye lends his name to an equally colorful perennial. In mid- to late summer, 2' to 5' stems carry large terminal clusters of dusty rose-colored flowers. Quilted, deep green, lance-shaped leaves are borne in tiered whorls of 4 to 6. Plants grow from stout, fibrous-rooted crowns. Found in low woods, open wet meadows, wet prairies and marshes. Zones: USDA 3-7, Sunset 1-11, 14-22.

Bottlebrush sedge, *Carex comosa*
Nodding, slender bottlebrush flowers are carried in open clusters amongst narrow, bright green leaves. Flowers resemble stiff caterpillars. Leaves form dense tufts from fibrous-rooted crowns. Plants prefer wet soil but will tolerate evenly moist soil that doesn't become too dry in summer. Blooms in late spring. Found in wet ditches, marshes, bogs and around lakes. Zones: USDA 3-8, Sunset 1-9, 14-24.

White Turtlehead

White turtlehead, *Chelone glabra*
Turtleheads delight gardeners with their unusual tubular flowers that look like a turtle with its mouth agape. White or pale purple flowers borne in terminal clusters and the upper leaf axils open for several weeks in late summer and autumn. Narrow, deep green leaves grow in pairs on 1' to 3' stems that sprout from fibrous-rooted crowns. Zones: USDA 4-8, Sunset 1-11, 14-22.

Water Willow

Bog Avens

Water willow, *Decodon verticillatus*

An open, sprawling shrub with arching stems that root when they touch water or soil, creating an illusion that the plant is walking on water. Leaves are brilliant green and willow-like. Bundles of small, rose-pink flowers are borne in whorls in the leaf axils. Easy to grow in any soil. May need restraining in open soil. Found in open bogs, wooded swamps and pond margins. Zones: USDA 3-9, Sunset 1-9, 14-24.

Bog bean, *Menyanthes trifoliata*

Trailing stems of bog bean float on open water or ramble through mosses and wetland sedges. Sea-green leaves are comprised of three oblong leaflets. In spring, naked stems crowned with a tight cluster of sweet-scented, fringed white flowers rise up to a foot above the leaves. Plant in bog gardens or in pots in pools and ponds. Found in open bogs, marshes and sluggish streams. Zones: USDA 2-7, Sunset 1-9, 14-21.

Bog avens, *Geum rivale*

In spring, the enchanting purple to creamy white flowers of bog avens nod on slender stems. Each flower is wrapped in hairy leaf-like bracts. Fading flowers give way to fuzzy, spherical seed heads. Soft, hairy, pinnately divided basal leaves reduce in size as they ascend the 1' to 1-1/2' stem. The plants grow from fibrous-rooted crowns. Found in wet woods, marshes and bogs. Zones: USDA 2-7, Sunset 1-9, 14-21.

Lotus, *Nelumbo lutea*

American lotus is the aristocrat of wetland plants. In mid-summer, tall naked stems rising high above the water sport huge yellow flowers. Decorative, flat-faced seed pods are perforated with Swiss cheese-like holes. Round leaves float on the water in spring, but summer's leaves stand out of the water on stiff stems. Plants adapt well to pot culture. Zones: USDA 4-9, Sunset all zones.

Sweet gale, *Myrica gale*

A showy, fragrant, deciduous shrub hardy in the far north. Rounded dense shrubs up to 5' tall, depending on the severity of the climate. Plants have 1" to 2-1/2", deep green shiny leaves. Under extreme conditions, plants may grow only a foot high. Yellowish fruits are carried in dense, short catkins. Found in bogs along streams and lake shores, and in wet dunes from Canada and Alaska, south to Virginia, Michigan and Washington. Zones: USDA 3-7, Sunset 1-7, 14-20.

Elderberry

Elderberry, *Sambucus canadensis*

Lovely shrub with glossy, pinnately compound leaves. Arching stems form an open crown up to 12' high with an equal spread. In early to mid-summer, 6" to 8" flattened lacy heads of creamy white flowers cover plant from top to bottom. Flowers give way to purple-black berries adored by birds. Edible flowers and fruits. Yellow fall foliage. Zones: USDA 3-9, Sunset 1-7, 14-17.

Softstem bulrush, *Scirpus*
tabernaemontani

Stiff, deep green, hollow leaves rise 3' to 9' above open water. Airy terminal clusters of small brown flowers borne from one side of the stem hang down like tassels. Flowers are produced in summer and early autumn. Plants spread from creeping rhizomes. Bulrushes form open stands in the shallow or deep water of marshes and ponds. Good nesting habitat for marsh birds. Zones: USDA 3-8, Sunset 1-7, 14-24.

Prairie Cordgrass

Prairie cordgrass, *Spartina pectinata*

Dense stands of bright green leaves sprout from creeping rhizomes. Leaf margins are razor sharp, giving the plant its well-deserved alternate common name — rip-gut. In summer, spikes up to 8' tall bear stiff flower clusters resembling thin combs. Leaves turn yellow and bronze in autumn. Best to contain growth in small water gardens to prevent plant from taking over. Found in wet ditches, low meadows and prairies and the edges of wetlands. Zones: USDA 3-8, Sunset 1-7, 14-24.

Marsh fern, *Thelypteris palustris*
Delicate, bright green fronds are twice-divided. They are carried on shiny black stipes up to 2' long. Often fronds are borne singly from creeping rhizomes, but where space permits plants form open clusters. Fronds turn yellow in autumn. Found in low woods, wet meadows and prairies, bogs and marshes. Zones: USDA 2-8, Sunset 2-7, 14-22.

Marsh marigold, *Caltha palustris*
A cheery early spring bloomer. Buttercup yellow blooms in multi-flower clusters open above dense rosettes of the round, scalloped edible leaves that double in size after the flowers fade.The entire clump goes dormant during the heat of summer. Plants grow from thick, fibrous-rooted crowns. Found in woodland streams, seepage slopes, shrub swamps and low woods. Zones: USDA 2-6, Sunset all zones.

MORE WETLAND PLANTS FOR

THE MIDWEST & GREAT PLAINS

TREES

Acer rubrum, Red maple
Acer saccharinum, Silver maple
Alnus incana ssp. *rugosa,* Speckled alder
Asimina triloba, Pawpaw
Betula nigra, River birch
Fraxinus nigra, Black ash
Larix laricina, Tamarack
Picea mariana, Black spruce
Quercus bicolor, Swamp white oak
Salix nigra, Black willow
Thuja occidentalis, White cedar

SHRUBS AND VINES

Andromeda polifolia ssp. *glaucophylla,*
    Bog rosemary
Chamaedaphne calyculata, Leatherleaf
Ledum groenlandicum, Labrador tea
Myrica gale, Sweet gale
Potentilla fruticosa, Shrubby cinquefoil
Spiraea tomentosa, Hardhack
Spiraea virginiana, Spirea
Viburnum dentatum, Arrowwood

PERENNIALS

Acorus calamus, Sweet flag
Alisma plantago-aquatica, Water plantain
Aster puniceus, Purple-stemmed aster

Aster lanceolatus var. *lanceolatus,* Marsh aster

Bidens cernua, Nodding bidens

Eupatorium perfoliatum, Boneset

Helenium autumnale, Sneezeweed

Helianthus grosseserratus, Big-toothed sunflower

Hibiscus moscheutos ssp. *lasiocarpos,* Marsh mallow

Hymenocallis caroliniana, Spider lily

Iris versicolor, Blue flag iris

Iris virginica, Virginia blue flag

Liatris pycnostachya, Prairie blazing star

Lobelia cardinalis, Cardinal flower

Lobelia spicata, Pale-spiked lobelia

Mimulus ringens, Monkey flower

Nuphar lutea ssp. *variegata,* Spadderdock

Nymphaea odorata, Water-lily

Orontium aquaticum, Golden-club

Parnassia glauca, Grass-of-Parnassus

Petasites frigidus, Coltsfoot

Physostegia virginiana, Obedient plant

Polygonum amphibium, Water smartweed

Pontederia cordata, Pickerel weed

Ranunculus flabellaris, Water buttercup

Sagittaria latifolia, Arrowhead

Sarracenia purpurea, Purple pitcher plant

Saururus cernuus, Lizard's tail

Saxifraga pensylvanica, Swamp saxifrage

Senecio aureus, Golden ragwort

Solidago spp., including *S. gigantea, S. ohioensis and S. riddellii*

Symplocarpus foetidus, Skunk cabbage

Veratrum viride, False hellebore

Verbena hastata, Blue vervain

Vernonia gigantea ssp. *gigantea,* Tall ironweed

Xyris spp., Yellow-eyed grasses

Zigadenus elegans, Death camas

GRASSES & GRASS-LIKE PLANTS

Carex comosa, Bottle sedge

Carex muskingumensis, Palm sedge

Carex pendula, Drooping sedge

Eriophorum vaginatum var. *spissum,* Cottongrass

Scirpus spp., Bulrushes

Sparganium spp., Bur reeds

Zizania aquatica, Wild rice

FERNS

Dryopteris cristata, Crested wood fern

Equisetum spp., Horsetails

Onoclea sensibilis, Sensitive fern

Osmunda cinnamomea, Cinnamon fern

Osmunda regalis, Royal fern

Woodwardia areolata, Netted chain fern

WETLAND PLANTS

For the Western Mountains & Pacific Northwest

BY DAN HINKLEY

THE TIDAL DUNES of the western coast, the hanging bogs of southern Oregon's steep mountainsides and the perpetually moist alpine meadows of Colorado each host an array of uniquely adapted plant species. However, throughout the vast region, a few species are commonly found at nearly all wetland sites. The dominant overstory trees include willows, alders and cottonwood. Beneath them, smaller willows, shrubby dogwoods and brambles including salmonberries often provide a secondary level of shrubs. At ground level are ferns, rushes and sedges. The soil in northwestern wetlands is characteristically acidic, and hence bogs are the prevalent wetland type.

Elk clover, *Aralia californica*
Herbaceous stems reaching up to 6' by mid-summer sport large compound leaves 3-1/2' long. Large panicles of white ball-shaped flower clusters at the end of each stem. Later in summer, resulting fruit ripens to a glossy black, causing each stem to arch gracefully downward. Foliage turns a lovely gold in autumn. Found in and along streams with *Darmera peltata*. Zones. USDA 4-8, Sunset 2-24.

Vine Maple

Goatsbeard

Vine maple, *Acer circinatum*
The only maple closely related to the Japanese maple occurring outside of Asia. Greenish stems rising to 20' bear handsome, roundish-lobed leaves that turn spectacular shades of orange and yellow in autumn in full sun. Grows anywhere from average garden soil through perpetually moist conditions. Vine maple is found throughout the Pacific Northwest in lowland shaded forests as well as high elevation mountain slopes. Zones: USDA 6-9, Sunset 1-6, 14-17.

Dwarf blue willow, *Salix purpurea*
  'Nana'
An extremely hardy shrub with finely textured leaves. Slender stems arch beautifully when weighted by summer rains. In winter, stems turn muted lavender. Small catkins are produced in very early spring. Easily forced indoors by cutting branches in late winter. Zones: USDA 3-7, Sunset all zones.

Goatsbeard, *Aruncus dioicus*
A superb and underutilized herbaceous perennial that grows in rich, moist soils in shade. Mounds of deeply cut, compound leaves to 4' give rise to tall panicles of airy white flowers to nearly 6', which gracefully nod at the tips. Though tolerant of full sun in very moist soils, fares better in partial to full shade. Found along road cuts and moist ravines across North America. Zones: USDA 3-8, Sunset all zones.

Twinberry, *Lonicera involucrata*
Pairs of yellow flowers held in a colorful red sepal, which swells and inflates as the twin blackish fruits ripen in late summer, grow along stems to 4' tall. Excellent autumn color. Found most commonly on flooded dunes adjacent to Pacific Ocean beaches. Zones: USDA 3-8, Sunset 5-9.

Sedge, *Carex obnupta*

Deep green sedge reaching to 18". Flowering stems sport elegantly drooping, golden flowers which rise to 2'. Vigorously self sows in moist soils. Provides an ideal waterside plant which will tolerate lowering water levels in mid- to late summer. Extremely tolerant of low light conditions. Equally at home in full sun if grown in moist soils. Zones: USDA 4-8, Sunset 4-9.

Red-osier Dogwood

Lady Fern

Lady fern, *Athyrium filix-femina*

Frilly and lacy fern that thrives in continually saturated soil. Produces clumps of erect fronds to 4'. At home in full sun or partial shade and will eagerly self sow in a moist location. Can easily spread. Commonly found in very moist areas, though can be accommodated by moderately moist soils as well. Zones: USDA 3-9, Sunset 14-24.

Red-osier dogwood, *Cornus stolonifera*

Red- or yellow-stemmed varieties are favorities for massing in wetland situations. Bark colors are most brilliant in winter. Cultivars with variegated leaves are available. Clusters of white flowers are followed by white berries. Frequently found in moist soils along rivers and streams throughout the West. Able to thrive in near-standing water. Zones: USDA 3-8, Sunset 3-9.

Umbrella plant, *Darmera peltata*

In earliest spring, clusters of delicate pink flowers appear on naked stems to 2', followed by pleated, rounded leaves which ultimately unfurl to 15" across on sturdy stems to 4'. Foliage is spectacular in autumn if grown in full sun. Umbrella plant is found along shaded streams in southern Oregon and northern California. Zones: USDA 4-7, Sunset 1-7, 14-20.

Salal

Salal, *Gaultheria shallon*
Ubiquitous Northwest evergreen shrub at home in moist and dry soils alike. Stems rising to 4' bear leathery evergreen foliage. Clusters of elegant, blushed white bells in late spring are followed by edible bluish black fruit in autumn. Found in a wide array of conditions, from upland dry sites to moist valley bottoms. Zones: USDA 7-9, Sunset 3-7, 14-17, 21-24.

Hardhack, *Spiraea douglasii*
Foliage is borne along erect 5' mahogany stems in early spring. Narrow leaves are bluish green on top and velvety white underneath. Conical heads of soft pink flowers emerge in early to mid June, forming 8" tall clusters in July and August. Found in dense thickets in winter-flooded areas of the Northwest. Zones: USDA 5-8, Sunset 1-11, 14-21.

Cattails, *Typha* spp.
Many species are available for cultivation, all of which make lovely, vigorous stands of deciduous foliage. In early spring, foliage is translucent green. Typical brown fruit held above or amongst the foliage appear later. Leaves turn magnificent yellow with the first frosts. Attract a number of bird species. Thrive in standing year-round or seasonal water. Zones: USDA 2-10, Sunset all zones.

Marsh Marigold

Marsh marigold, *Caltha leptosepala*
Lesser known ornamental species that thrives at water's edge in western mountains. Lovely white flowers bloom in early spring just as the snows melt. Does well in garden settings and deserves more recognition as a superb moisture-loving species. Zones: USDA 4-7, Sunset 5-9.

Skunk Cabbage

Western Azalea

Skunk cabbage, *Lysichiton americanus*

A highly ornamental plant despite its off-putting and somewhat misleading common name. In early spring, hooded yellow flowers arise from emerging rosettes of foliage. As the flowers fade, leaves expand to 3' under optimal conditions of near standing water. Skunk cabbage tolerates full sun or shade. Zones: USDA 6-8, Sunset 6-9.

Western azalea, *Rhododendron occidentale*

Offers lovely and very fragrant white flowers, spotted with yellow, in mid- to late summer when little else is in bloom. A parent of many hardy hybrid azaleas in cultivation, this species is among the royalty of the genus. Best grown in very moist situations in partial shade or full sun. Native to southern Oregon and northern California. Zones: USDA 6-8, Sunset 6-9.

MORE WETLAND PLANTS FOR

THE WESTERN MOUNTAINS & PACIFIC NORTHWEST

TREES

Acer rubrum, Red maple
Betula nigra, River birch
Betula papyrifera, Paper birch
Cornus alternifolia, Pagoda dogwood
Nyssa sylvatica, Sour gum
Taxodium distichum, Bald cypress

SHRUBS

Aronia arbutifolia, Aronia
Cephalanthus occidentalis, Buttonbush
Clethra alnifolia, Sweet pepperbush
Cornus alba, Red twig dogwood
Cornus racemosa, Gray dogwood
Ilex verticillata and cultivars,
   Winterberry holly
Magnolia virginiana, Sweet bay magnolia
Rubus spectabilis, Salmon berry
Salix elaeagnos, Rosemary willow
Zanthoxylum americanum, Toothache
   tree

PERENNIALS

Astilbe biternata, False goat's beard
Cardamine pratensis, Lady's smock
Cimicifuga laciniata, Oregon bugbane
Corydalis scouleri, Corydalis
Dactylorhiza maculata, Spotted ground
   orchid
Darlingtonia californica, Cobra lily
Equisetum hyemale, Evergreen horsetail
Geranium maculatum, Wild geranium
Iris pseudacorus, Yellow flag
Matteuccia struthiopteris, Ostrich fern
Mimulus ringens, Allegheny monkey
   flower
Miscanthus floridulus, Eulalia
Polygonum bistorta 'Superba', Snakeweed
Primula vulgaris, Common primrose
Ranunculus ficaria, Lesser celandine
Typha angustifolia, Narrowleaf cattail
Vaccinium oxycoccus, Small cranberry
Veratrum californicum, California false
   hellebore, Corn lilly

WETLAND PLANTS

For California

BY ROBYN S. MENIGOZ

CALIFORNIA IS VAST, including a wide range of moisture levels, topography and soils, which determine the overall pattern of wetlands. Rainfall progressively decreases from north to south. Mountain ranges have more rain on seaward than on eastward sides. The far northern part of the state has a few pitcher plant bogs. Most freshwater marshes are in the central portion of the state. The riparian woodlands that once predominated throughout the state have been dammed or diverted. In southernmost California, seasonal streams or washes are common. The best time to plant in California is in the fall, when it is still warm enough to promote root growth and impending winter rains will keep the new root growth watered.

Pipevine, *Aristolochia californica*
A twining vine sporting curious, light green, pipe-like blooms with purple venation that appear in late winter before the heart-shaped leaves unfurl. Important host plant for the pipevine swallowtail butterfly. Found in shady ravines and along streambanks below 1500'. Grows best in partial shade. Zones: USDA 8, Sunset 7-9, 14-24.

California black-flowering sedge,
    Carex nudata
A clumping deciduous sedge that turns bright yellow and orange before going dormant. Soft brown foliage persists on the plant during the winter. Come spring, the fresh gray-green foliage is topped with showy black flowers held on upright spikes 18" to 24" above the foliage. Will grow in

shallow water or moist, fertile soil in full sun to deep shade. Zones: USDA 8, Sunset 4-9, 14-24.

Western Spicebush

Western spicebush,
Calycanthus occidentalis

A bold, handsome, fast-growing shrub native to year-round streams in cool, coastal mid-mountain forests. Dark green leaves turn light yellow in autumn. Showy maroon "water-lily" flowers smell of wine barrels — a nice complement to the shredding bark that smells of allspice. Large, goblet-shaped seed pods add winter interest. Grows in full sun on the coast and in dappled shade inland. Zones: USDA 7, Sunset 4-9, 14-22.

Hazelnut, *Corylus cornuta* var. *californica*

A fast-growing, large, deciduous shrub found along damp slopes and banks below 7000'. In late winter, long, slender golden beige tassels decorate the horizontally layered branches. Broad, heart-shaped, bright green leaves glow in dappled shade. Wildlife relish the nuts in early fall. Provide filtered shade and consistent water. Zones: USDA 7, Sunset 1-9, 14-20

Stream Orchid

Stream orchid, *Epipactis gigantea*

New shoots of lanceolate leaves emerge in late spring from this winter-dormant perennial. Loose racemes of purple-red orchid flowers bloom from late spring to early summer. Tough roots seek out damp crevices in rocks and naturalize throughout the water course. Provide year-round moisture with good drainage and dappled shade. Commonly found along moist streambanks below 7500'. Zones: USDA 7, Sunset 8-24.

California Gray Rush

Leopard Lily

California gray rush, *Juncus patens*

A somewhat stiff, dense fountain of slender blue-green stems about 2' tall, this rush is an ideal accent for shady, moist spots. Grows in shallow water where it makes an interesting ground-cover massed along the water's edge. Prefers moist fertile soil in light shade, but will tolerate full sun as long as moisture is present. Zones: USDA 8, Sunset 8-24.

California polypody,
   Polypodium californicum

An attractive summer-dormant fern with deeply divided foot-tall fronds. Creeping rhizomes in early fall give rise to bright green fronds that last into spring. A hybrid form with dark evergreen fronds is available. Grows well among rocks along the water's edge, conditions similar to those in its native habitat of shady banks and cliffs throughout the coast ranges. Zones: USDA 8, Sunset 4-9, 14-17, 20-24.

Leopard lily, *Lilium pardalinum*

The grace of this perennial belies its vigorous growth. Creeping rhizomes establish colonies along streamsides in forests or open seeps. Stout 5' stems with whorled leaves hold loose clusters of nodding red or orange blossoms. Reflexed petals spotted with dark maroon bloom from May to July. Plant in sun or part shade near the coast, part shade inland. Provide continuous moisture. Zones: USDA 7, Sunset all zones.

Fremont cottonwood, *Populus*
   fremontii

This broad, open-crown tree grows to a height of 50' feet or more. Heart-shaped, light green leaves reflect the light and turn a clear pale yellow in autumn. White upright trunk is showy against the gray winter sky. Flattened leafstalks catch the wind, setting the leaves in motion with the slightest breeze. A good specimen for the wetland garden, it grows in moist areas below 6500'. Zones: USDA 8, Sunset 7-24.

Ninebark*, Physocarpus capitatus*
A fast-growing 3'- to 7'-tall shrub that is attractive year-round. In mid-spring, branches are covered with rose pink buds that become dense clusters of small, white flowers. A red, capsular fruit follows. Autumn leaves fall away to reveal brownish bark peeling away from the older branches. Younger twigs are reddish in color. Distinctive leaves are rounded, slightly lobed and coarsely toothed. Grows best in shade along moist banks and north slopes below 4500'. Needs some pruning to look its best in the garden. Zones: USDA 5, Sunset 1-3, 10.

Yellow tree willow, *Salix lucida*
  ssp. *lasiandra*
An attractive, graceful, streamside tree that grows to 20' to 50' high. Seven inch-long, tapered, shiny, dark green leaves move freely in the wind. Young yellow branches contrast nicely with dark brown, rough bark of trunk and older branches. Blooms from March through July. Female trees produce showier blooms. Found along stream-banks and moist places below 8000' where its network of roots help slow erosion. Zones: USDA 7, Sunset 4-9, 14-24.

California grape, *Vitis californica*
A woody vine capable of growing up to 50' long. Large, softly lobed leaves create a lush green curtain of growth with curling tendrils that attach to support structures. Small greenish yellow, fragrant flowers produce dark purple grapes that contrast nicely with yellow, crimson and flame-red autumn foliage. A good plant for wildlife. Prefers filtered sun in riparian areas below 1500'. Zones: USDA 7, Sunset 7-9, 14-24.

Primrose Monkeyflower

Primrose monkeyflower, *Mimulus primuloides*
Barely five inches tall, this diminutive evergreen perennial forms a mat-like carpet of bright green at the water's edge. From June to August it is covered with bright yellow flowers held well above the foliage. Grows easily in wet soil and either sun or light shade. Zones: USDA 8, Sunset 7-24.

Chain fern, *Woodwardia fimbriata*
Found along streamsides and moun-

tain seeps, this striking fern has upright, light green fronds from 4' to 8' long. Fronds made up of coarse large segments persist until the new fronds uncoil. Old fronds should be removed as new ones unfurl. Chain fern is a tough, giant fern that tolerates many soils and requires partial shade with moisture. Zones: USDA 7, Sunset 4-9, 14-24.

California Fan Palm

California fan palm,
Washingtonia filifera
A beautiful palm reaching 45' to 60'. Sturdy, column-like trunk clothed with a brown thatch skirt of old fronds sports a head of fan-shaped, gray-green 3' to 6' fronds. In June, 12' panicles of creamy white flowers perfume the air. Found along alkaline seeps, springs and streams in arid climates of southern California. Requires full sun and ample moisture. Zones: USDA 9, Sunset 8-10 (warmer parts), 11-24.

MORE WETLAND PLANTS FOR CALIFORNIA

TREES

Acer circinatum, Vine maple
Acer glabrum, Sierra maple
Acer macrophyllum, Bigleaf maple
Alnus rhombifolia, White alder
Betula occidentalis, Water birch
Chilopsis linearis, Desert willow
Platanus racemosa, Western sycamore
Quercus lobata, Valley oak
Salix laevigata, Red willow
Umbellularia californica, California bay

SHRUBS AND VINES

Clematis ligusticifolia, Virgin's bower
Cornus stolonifera, American dogwood
Euonymus occidentalis, Western burning bush
Lonicera hispidula var. *vacillans,* Honeysuckle
Myrica californica, Wax myrtle
Philadelphus lewisii, Mock orange
Physocarpus capitatus, Ninebark
Rhamnus purshiana, Cascara sagrada
Rhododendron macrophyllum, California rhododendron
Rhododendron occidentale, Western azalea
Ribes sanguineum, Red flowering currant
Rosa californica, California wild rose

Rubus spectabilis, Salmon berry
Salix hindsiana, Sandbar willow
Styrax officinalis, Californica snowdrop
   bush
Vaccinium ovatum, California
   huckleberry

PERENNIALS

Aquilegia formosa, Red columbine
Aralia californica, Elk clover
Darlingtonia californica, Pitcher plant
Darmera peltata, Indian rhubarb
Delphinium glaucum, Tower delphinium
Dicentra formosa, Pacific bleeding heart
Dodecatheon dentatum, Shooting star
Drosera rotundifolia, Sundew
Heracleum lanatum, Cow parsnip
Heuchera micrantha, Alum root
Lobelia cardinalis, Cardinal flower
Lysichiton americanus, Skunk cabbage
Maianthemum dilatatum, False lily-of-
   the-valley
Mimulus cardinalis, Scarlet
   monkeyflower
Mimulus guttatus, Monkey flower
Mitella ovalis, Bishop's-cap
Oxalis oregana, Redwood sorrel
Petasites frigidus var. *palmatus,* Western
   coltsfoot
Rudbeckia californica, Coneflower
Sambucus racemosa, Red elderberry
Sidalcea oregana ssp. *spicata,* Oregon
   sidalcea
Sisyrinchium bellum, Blue-eyed grass

Smilacina racemosa, Branched
   Solomon's seal
Smilacina stellata, Star Solomon's seal
Spiraea douglasii, Spiraea
Symphoricarpos albus var. *laevigatus,*
   Snowberry
Tolmiea menziesii, Tolmiea
Veratrum californicum, Corn lily

GRASSES AND GRASS-LIKE PLANTS

Anemopsis californica, Yerba mansa
Carex tumulicola, Berkeley sedge
Deschampsia cespitosa, Hairgrass
Eriophorum gracile, Slender cotton grass
Juncus balticus, Baltic rush
Parnassia californica, Grass-of-Parnassus
Typha domingensis, Cattail

FERNS

Adiantum pedatum, Five finger fern
Athyrium filix-femina var. *cyclosorum,*
   Lady fern
Blechnum spicant, Deer fern
Polypodium californicum, California
   polypody
Polystichum munitum, Western sword
   fern

NURSERY SOURCES

BITTERROOT RESTORATION
445 Quast Lane
Corvalis, MT 59828
(406) 961-4991
free catalog

BLACKLEDGE RIVER NURSERY
155 Jerry Daniels Road
Marlborough, CT 06447
(860) 295-1022
free catalog

CAL FLORA
P.O. Box 3
Fulton, CA 95439
(707) 528-8813
(no mail order)

ENVIRONMENTAL CONCERN
PO Box P
St. Michaels, MD 21663
(410) 745-9620
free catalog

FLYING COW FARMS
16361 Norris Road
Laxahatchee, FL 33470
(561) 790-1422
free catalog

FOREST FARM NURSERY
990 Tetherow Road
Williams, OR 97544-9599
(541) 846-7269
catalog $4

FRESHWATER FARMS
5851 Myrtle Avenue
Eureka, CA 95503
(707)444-8261
(800) 200-8969
free catalog

FROSTY HOLLOW
Box 53
Langley, WA 98260
(360) 579-2332
free seed list with SASE

GENESIS NURSERY
23200 Hurd Road
Tampico, IL 61283
(815) 438-2220
free catalog

GOSSLER FARMS NURSERY
1200 Weaver Road
Springfield, OR 97478-9691
(541) 746-3922
catalog $2

HERONSWOOD NURSERY
7530 N.E. 288th Street
Kingston, WA 98346-9502
(360) 297-4172
catalog $4/ 2-year subscription

McALLISTER WATER GARDENS
7420 St. Helena Highway
Yountville, CA 94599
(707) 944-0921
free catalog

NEW ENGLAND WETLAND PLANTS
800 Main Street
Amherst, MA 01002
(413) 256-1752
free catalog, wholesale only

NICHE GARDENS
1111 Dawson Road
Chapel Hill, NC 27516
(919) 967-0078
free catalog

NORTH CREEK NURSERIES
R.R. 2, Box 33
Landenberg, PA 19350
(610) 255-0100
Free catalog

PINELANDS NURSERY
323 Island Road
Columbus, NJ 08022
(800) 667-2729
free catalog, retail by
appointment only

PLANT DELIGHTS NURSERY
9241 Sauls Road
Raleigh, NC 27603
(919) 772-4794
free catalog

PRAIRIE RESTORATIONS
31922-128th Street
Princeton, MN 55371
(612) 389-4342

PRAIRIE RIDGE NURSERY
9738 Overland Road
Mt. Horeb, WI 53572-2823
(608) 437-5245
catalog $3, refundable
with purchase

SARATOGA HORTICULTURAL RESEARCH FOUNDATION
15185 Murphy Avenue
San Martin, CA 95046
(408) 779-3303
free availability list

SOUTHERN TIER
2677 Route 305
P.O. Box 30
West Clarksville, NY 14786
(800) 848-7614
free catalog

TEMPLE UNIVERSITY NATIVE PLANT NURSERY
Department of
Landscape
Architecture and
Horticulture
Ambler, PA 19002-3994
(215) 283-1330
free price list

TREE OF LIFE
33201 Ortega Highway
San Juan Capistrano, CA 92675
(714) 728-0685
(no mail order)

WATER WAYS NURSERY
13015 Milltown Road
Lovettsville, VA 20180
(540) 822-5994
catalog $2

WILD EARTH NATIVE PLANT NURSERY
49 Mead Avenue
Freehold, NJ 07728
(908) 308-9777
catalog $2

YERBA BUENA NURSERY
19500 Skyline Boulevard
Woodside, CA 94062
(415) 851-1668
availability list $2

CONTRIBUTORS

THOMAS BENJAMIN is a landscape architect and bioengineering consultant based in Sommerville, Massachussetts. He has managed a number of bioengineering projects over the past decade.

C. COLSTON BURRELL is a garden designer, writer, photographer and life-long native plant enthusiast. He is president of Native Landscape Design and Restoration, Ltd. of Minneapolis, Minnesota, a design firm specializing in the creation of environmentally appropriate gardens and restorations.

LOGAN CALHOUN is a landscape architect and plantsman based in Dallas, Texas. He travels throughout North America looking for superior plants for garden use. He is also co-founder of King's Creek Landscaping and Gardens.

CAROL FRANKLIN, a founding member of Andropogon Associates, Ltd. in Philadelphia, Pennsylvania, is an ecological planner and designer. Andropogon specializes in restoration, re-creation and management of natural habitas.

SUSAN GALATOWITSCH is assistant professor of landscape ecology at the University of Minnesota in the departments of Horticultural Science and Landscape Architecture. She is co-author of *Restoring Prairie Wetlands: An Ecological Approach* (Iowa State University Press).

JUDY GLATTSTEIN is a garden consultant, a garden writer and a popular speaker in the U.S. and abroad. She has authored four books, including *Waterscaping: Plants and Ideas for Natural and Created Water Gardens* (Storey Communications).

DAN HINKLEY gardens on 7-1/2 acres on the North Kitsap Peninsula across the Puget Sound from Seattle, and with his partner, Robert Jones, operates a small mail order nursery called Heronswood.

ROBYN S. MENIGOZ is a landscape architect based in Novato, California. She has designed many award-winning gardens in the San Francisco Bay Area, all with a focus on native plants and habitats.

FRED ROZUMALSKI practices ecosystem restoration in the Minneapolis/St. Paul area. He holds degrees in horticulture, ecology and landscape architecture. Currently, he is a research fellow at the University of Minnesota investigating wetland vegetation regeneration.

GEORGIA TASKER is garden writer for *The Miami Herald* and author of *Wild Things: The Return of Native Plants* (Florida Native Plant Society, 1982, out of print) and *Enchanted Ground: Gardening With Nature in the Subtropics* (Andrews and McMeel, 1994).

CRAIG TUFTS is chief naturalist and oversees the Backyard Habitat program for the National Wildlife Federation. He is the author of *The Backyard Naturalist* (National Wildlife Federation, 1987) and co-author with Peter Loewer of *The National Wildlife Federation's Guide to Gardening for Wildlife* (Rodale, 1994).

LESLIE YETKA of the University of Minnesota Department of Horticultural Science, holds an M.S. in Horticultural Science with a minor in water resources. For the past seven years, she has conducted research on revegetating sedge meadows in created and restored wetlands, and on the plant ecology of peatlands.

ILLUSTRATION CREDITS

Drawings by STEVE BUCHANAN
Cover photo and pages 5, 6, 20, 21, 24, 25, 27, 54, 55, 76 and 78 by DEREK FELL; pages 1, 46 left and right, 47 left and right and 95 left by SUSAN GLASCOCK; pages 8 left and 94 right by MARK TURNER; pages 8 right, 10 and 75 right by CHRISTINE M. DOUGLAS; pages 9 left and right, 12, 13, 15, 30 left, 33 left and right, 49, 50, 51, 52, 53, 69 left, 75 left, 87 left and right, 88 left, 89 right, 93 right, 94 left, 95 right and 96 left and right by C. COLSTON BURRELL; page 30 right by DIANA LOBIEN; page 14 by ALAN and LINDA DETRICK; pages 37, 38, 39, 40 left and right and 41 by ANDROPOGON ASSOCIATES; pages 44 and 45 by CRAIG TUFTS; pages 58, 59, 61, 62, 63 and 66 left, right and bottom by DON KNEZICK; pages 69 right, 70 left and right, 71 left and right and 72 by JUDY GLATTSTEIN; pages 77, 81 left, 82 right and 83 by ROGER L. HAMMER; pages 81 right, 82 left and 84 by GEORGIA TASKER; pages 88 right and 89 left by PAMELA HARPER; page 93 left by ROBYN S. MENIGOZ; pages 99 left and 102 by BOB PERRY; pages 99 right and 101 by TED KIPPING; page 100 left by SAXON HOLT; page 100 right by MICHAEL S. THOMPSON.

INDEX

Gardening Books
FOR THE
Next Century

Published four times a year,
these award-winning books explore the
frontiers of ecological gardening.
Your subscription to BBG's **21st-Century
Gardening Series** is free with
Brooklyn Botanic Garden membership.

TO BECOME A MEMBER

please call (718) 622-4433, ext. 265.
Or, photocopy this form,
complete and return to:
Membership Department, Brooklyn Botanic Garden,
1000 Washington Avenue, Brooklyn, NY 11225-1099

YOUR NAME . . . .

ADDRESS . . . .

CITY/STATE/ZIP . . . .

PHONE . . . .

I want to subscribe to the 21st-Century Gardening Series
(4 quarterly volumes) by becoming a member of the
Brooklyn Botanic Garden:

☐ **$35 · SUBSCRIBER**   ☐ **$125 · SIGNATURE**

☐ **$50 · FAMILY/DUAL**   ☐ **$300 · SPONSOR**

TOTAL $ . . . .

FORM OF PAYMENT:

☐ CHECK ENCLOSED ☐ VISA ☐ MASTERCARD

CREDIT CARD# . . . .

EXP . . . .

SIGNATURE . . . .

FOR INFORMATION ON ORDERING
ANY OF THE FOLLOWING BACK
TITLES, PLEASE WRITE THE
BROOKLYN BOTANIC GARDEN OR
CALL (718) 622-4433, EXT. 274.

AMERICAN COTTAGE GARDENING
ANNUALS: A GARDENER'S GUIDE
BONSAI: SPECIAL TECHNIQUES
BULBS FOR INDOORS
BUTTERFLY GARDENS
CULINARY HERBS
EASY-CARE ROSES
THE ENVIRONMENTAL GARDENER
FERNS
GARDEN PHOTOGRAPHY
THE GARDENER'S WORLD OF BULBS
GARDENING FOR FRAGRANCE
GARDENING IN THE SHADE
GARDENING WITH WILDFLOWERS
    & NATIVE PLANTS
GOING NATIVE: BIODIVERSITY
    IN OUR OWN BACKYARDS
GREENHOUSES & GARDEN ROOMS
GROWING FRUITS
HERBS & COOKING
HERBS & THEIR ORNAMENTAL USES
HOLLIES: A GARDENER'S GUIDE
INDOOR BONSAI
INVASIVE PLANTS
JAPANESE GARDENS
NATIVE PERENNIALS
THE NATURAL LAWN
NATURAL INSECT CONTROL
A NEW LOOK AT VEGETABLES
A NEW LOOK AT HOUSEPLANTS
ORCHIDS FOR THE HOME
    & GREENHOUSE
ORNAMENTAL GRASSES
PERENNIALS: A GARDENER'S GUIDE
PRUNING TECHNIQUES
ROSES
SALAD GARDENS
SHRUBS: THE NEW GLAMOUR PLANTS
SOILS
TANTALIZING TOMATOES
THE TOWN & CITY GARDENER
TREES: A GARDENER'S GUIDE
WATER GARDENING
THE WINTER GARDEN
WOODLAND GARDENS